Flying Fear Free

Flying Fear Free

7 Steps to Relieving Air Travel Anxiety

Sandra M. Pollino, M.S.Ed., Psy.D.

New Horizon Press
Far Hills, New Jersey

Pollino, Sandra M.
Flying Fear Free: 7 Steps to Relieving Air Travel Anxiety
Cover design: Wendy Bass
Interior design: Susan Sanderson

Library of Congress Control Number: 2011928839

ISBN-13: 978-0-88282-373-7
New Horizon Press

Manufactured in the U.S.A.

16 15 14 13 12 1 2 3 4 5

To Noelle, my daughter and best friend,
who has patiently supported my understanding
of the fear of flying, years of research
and development of a successful program.
I thank her for contributing her medical knowledge.

And to Angie, my mother, first editor and biggest fan.
She has given me her support from the start.

I love you both.

Author's Note

This book is based on the author's research, personal experiences, clients' real life experiences and information from members of the airline and mental health industries. In order to protect privacy, names have been changed and identifying characteristics have been altered except for contributing experts.

Any self-help book has its limitations and you should consult a physician or mental health professional if your situation is severe. Some of the therapies explained in this book have not been validated by empirical research but have proven successful for the author's clients and for the clients of many other professionals in the mental health field.

Statements regarding nutritional or health benefits of various substances are the opinions of the author. You should consult a physician or nutritionist prior to any dietary modifications.

Contents

Introduction

Fear of flying, also referred to as aviophobia, aerophobia, aviatophobia, flight fear or flight phobia, is the second most common phobia in the United States. There are approximately twenty-five million people in the United States who are anxious about flying. Among the millions reluctant to fly are public figures, business professionals, mothers, fathers and many others from all walks of life around the world.

Many fearful individuals stay awake at night at just the thought of air travel. These fearful flyers avoid flying and cancel flights. If they do make a flight, they fly with extreme discomfort and anxiety. The fear of flying may cause individuals to lose their jobs or to miss important family events.

After the tragic events on September 11, 2001, many individuals developed a fear of flying and shared their heartbreaking stories with me. I use an eclectic approach that has proven successful for treating individuals who are fearful of flying, utilizing theories which I have found are most effective for each individual. The most successful is Cognitive-Behavioral Therapy (CBT), a type of psychotherapy which decreases destructive emotions by correcting distorted thoughts and encourages healthy behavior. In conjunction with CBT, I use a holistic approach to treat the whole person, not just the problem.

As airplanes get older and we hear of more problems with air travel such as crashes, terrorists and sleeping air traffic controllers, fearful flyers continue to increase in number. Many programs and books on this subject fail to build courage in a fearful flyer and lack the necessary information to reduce anxiety. In *Flying Fear Free,* I list the techniques and procedures of a holistic approach that is proven to eliminate fear. This book enables you to want to fly, enjoy the flight and look forward to your next flight.

This Book Can Help You:

- Save your job
- Go to important events
- Improve your marriage
- Make family vacations possible and affordable

- Be there in time for a birth or death
- Save lives during an emergency evacuation
- Attend job conferences or conventions
- Get to concerts, athletic events and government assignments
- Conquer the fear and anxiety that can accompany air travel

As a nurse and flight attendant, I realized the need for research and a strong program to help fearful flyers, so I decided to return to college and further my education in psychology with this purpose in mind. As a flight attendant, I spent many flights using not only my airline training, but also my nursing training to help fearful flyers. These fearful flyers were most appreciative, but I knew there was more I could do. Since then, I have helped thousands overcome their fear of flying with my unique background as a nurse, psychotherapist, professor of psychology, performance coach and flight attendant.

I have presented programs on the fear of flying to corporations, government employees, educational institutions, sports teams and many more organizations. After 9/11, I helped anxious government officials board planes to return home to their worried loved ones. As a psychotherapist, I have successfully helped fearful flyers through group and individual counseling sessions and reality flights. The trust my clients have put in me and my background has allowed the program to grow with success. Some readers will still need counseling and perhaps medication, but there are millions who could be successful flyers if they had the complete package that this book offers.

I've been interviewed on television and radio talk shows, newspapers and more. I've been asked by many to write a self-help book for those suffering with the fear of flying. I fervently believe *Flying Fear Free* can be the support that fearful flyers need.

My Proven Approach to Conquering Flight Fear:

- Explains the causes of fear of flying
- Defines phobias
- Tells what to expect on a flight
- Gives details of air transportation
- Offers specific and easy techniques, exercises and procedures

- States statistics and facts regarding air travel
- Lists what foods should be eaten and not eaten during flights
- Describes what to wear and how to pack
- Explores how to use aromatherapy, color therapy, music therapy and dream therapy with empirical support
- Presents Cognitive-Behavioral Therapy and holistic techniques
- Demonstrates effective psychological, physical, emotional and spiritual techniques
- Shares fun exercises and checklists that help relieve stress and fear
- Helps the reader design an effective flight plan
- Aids in goal setting
- Shows how to select a support person
- Provides simple relaxation tips for tense muscles
- Interprets air travel industry practices, flights, planes, procedures, safety, etc.
- Reveals important skills other programs have left out

Common Causes of the Fear of Flying:

- **Aviophobia** or **Aerophobia**: Fear that during air travel the plane will crash and one will die
- **Agoraphobia**: Fear of being around people or away from home
- **Claustrophobia**: Fear of being in closed spaces
- **Acrophobia**: Fear of heights
- **Social Phobia**: Fear of being exposed to unfamiliar people or situations
- **Panic Attacks**: Fear of experiencing a panic attack on the plane
- **Control**: Fear of giving up control to the pilot
- **The Unknown**: Fear of not having an understanding of the airplane, flight crew or airline industry
- **Terrorists**: Fear due to a terrorist attack like 9/11 or a hijacking of the plane

- **Illness**: Fear that one may become ill in-flight and not be able to receive needed medical treatment in time
- **Bad Experience**: Problems on a former flight (e.g. turbulence)
- **Natural Disasters**: Fear of earthquake, flood, hurricane, tornado, tsunami, volcano
- **Superstition and Premonition**: Fear of flying on Friday the thirteenth or dreams of crashing

Overcoming the Fear of Flying

One out of every six American adults and millions more across the world are afraid of flying; many find it difficult to overcome their fears. Are you one of the many for whom air travel seems impossible? If so, you are not alone.

Here are some of the reasons why it may be difficult to overcome anxiety about air travel:

1. **Embarrassment**: You may feel embarrassed to admit that you are afraid to fly in an airplane. You will not seek help due to the embarrassment, seeing yourself as weak and wondering why others have no problem with air travel. Unfortunately, many friends and family members do not understand your fear. You may have heard questions and comments like, "What's wrong with you? There's nothing to it!" This only causes you to try to hide your fear and accumulate more stress.

2. **Multiple fears:** Most individuals with a fear of flying also have other fears. Along with a specific phobia (fear of flying), you may also be acrophobic, claustrophobic, etc. Many have lost faith in the safety of the industry. The anxiety you feel may cause an uncomfortable flight or shut you off from the thought of air travel.

Time spent on treatment: Some fearful flyers lament the time it will take to overcome their fear. But research has found that gradual exposure to fearful objects or situations is effective for extinguishing fear. It's called Progressive Desensitization. I help my clients design a flight plan, which takes them from the beginning to the end of their flights. The exposure includes education on the airline industry, films, simulated flights, visualization of a relaxed and safe flight and airport visits (with security clearance and prior arrangements made to observe, take a cognitive walk through the procedures, talk with pilots and board parked planes).

3. **Gaps in flight history:** A long period since your last flight can create anxiety. To lower your anxiety, it helps to take more frequent flights. Many do not have the time or money to do so, but there are some great discounted fares offered by some airlines. Take the time and treat yourself to a cheap and relaxing flight.

4. **Difficulty during a former flight:** You may recall the discomfort you experienced on a past flight, which caused you to feel uneasy or even suffer from Post-Traumatic Stress Disorder (PTSD). Understanding what caused your discomfort and working through the fear with the techniques and exercises in this book will help you fly free of fear.

5. **Stress in your life prior to flying:** Feeling stressed due to something that may have happened earlier in the day or week can contribute to the fear of flying. You may have other worries that cause you to be more sensitive towards an event like air travel. To relieve stress, it helps to take a deep breath in and let out all the built-up stress. You'll learn several techniques to relieve stress in this book.

6. **Media saturation:** Many individuals are afraid to fly because of erroneous messages from the media that air travel is unsafe. The media will feature a crash for days, even if only one or two people are involved. You don't see every automobile accident televised, yet airline incidents that should be minor or non-events are publicized for extended periods. You begin to associate the greater exposure and publicity about the problem with your sense of how critical the problem actually is.

7. **Perception of danger:** Education on the airline industry is a key factor in curing yourself from the fear of flying. Your perception of risk can make a difference. In *Flying Fear Free,* you'll learn that air travel is one of the safest means of transportation.

Learning How to Fly Without Fear

This book can help anyone who is motivated to work on overcoming their fear of flying. It can help families take and enjoy vacations, attend family events or visit a sick relative. It will benefit professionals who must travel for their jobs. And it will prepare you in case you must take air travel to escape harm in an evacuation or medical situation.

It can be painful to encounter this fear, but you are not alone. This book gives support for those who suffer from flight fear and for the professionals who want to help their many clients who present with this common problem. Some tasks to accomplish to fly comfortably are learning to trust the airline industry, accepting your feelings, using relaxation exercises and techniques, taking positive action and learning what to do with your worries. You will be given the tools to take these steps in *Flying Fear Free.*

How to Use This Book

The exercises and techniques in this book are designed to be easy and quickly accessible to you. Do the exercises thoughtfully. Even if you think some exercises are silly, the fact is they work! As you do the exercises, you'll discover that some may work better than others for you. Having a supply of exercises and techniques to use helps to build the courage you need to fly comfortably. In each chapter you'll find key facts and helpful review questions that you will want to jot down and take with you on every flight.

Along with the helpful exercises, this book will help you understand the fear of flying. You will find answers to your common questions like, "Why is this happening to me?" "What is wrong with me?" "Am I the only one afraid to fly?" "How am I ever going to get on that plane?" "How do I explain that my fear is real?"

For this book to work you need to set and embrace the goal of flying fear free. Any self-help has its limitations. Understand these limitations and realize when professional intervention is needed. You must be willing to listen to yourself, work hard and engage with the program.

This book assumes that you are in good enough emotional health to work on your fear of flying. Severe mental illnesses, substance addictions, anger management issues or personality disorders require professional intervention before the techniques in this book can be applied. Also, certain medical problems require consulting with your physician before some techniques in this book can be utilized.

A positive approach to everyday situations can not only lower your stress and anxiety levels, but also assist you in enjoying life to its fullest. It may be difficult to experience certain things in life, like flight fear, but it is how you cope with those challenges that will make you grow as a person. Everyone has the freedom to make choices; making choices promotes change and change promotes a happy, healthier lifestyle.

It is up to you to motivate yourself and make this book work for you. You can and you will! Become your own coach and use this book when you need assistance.

Relax. Take a deep breath in. Think only positive thoughts of an enjoyable flight. Now exhale, letting go of any unwelcome fear. It is time to tell your fear that you are dismissing it, because it has overstayed its welcome. Let's prepare to work hard while enjoying the program, and be free to fly without any worry or fear. What do you have to lose besides a wonderful vacation, an unforgettable honeymoon, the birth of your grandchild? What do you have to lose besides the moments of a lifetime?

Now let's move forward to finally *Flying Fear Free*!

PART I

Causes and Symptoms of Flight Fear

chapter 1

Getting Motivated

chapter goals:

To address the definition of fear, explore the "What Ifs?" and help you discover and understand why you are afraid to fly.

To help you become familiar with your own anxious feelings so you can successfully utilize the "Seven Steps to Flying More Comfortably."

For this program to work, you must stay positive and motivated to use the techniques in this book. Don't let yourself drift into the "What Ifs?" It is imperative that you begin to make changes to those negative thoughts of *I can't and I won't* and replace them with *I can and I will!* You must develop faith in yourself and in this self-help program to be successful.

Fear of flying is real and significant, but you can work to overcome your fear and have fun doing so. Yes, *fun*—a word that most fearful flyers don't associate with their thoughts of flying. But the first step in flying fear free is changing your attitude and the misconceptions you have about air travel. Instead of feeling anxiety when you see an airplane, start conditioning yourself to think of how beautiful and relaxing air travel can be. Think about how fortunate we are to have air travel, which is one of the safest means of transportation. Think about the perils of ground transportation: inclement weather, traffic, accidents, gas prices, etc. Condition yourself to say "I can and I will!" at least once every day, especially when negative thoughts enter your mind.

Kelly's Story

Kelly was a surgeon who worked hard to save lives and had no problem operating on patients. Her husband was a physician too, working in the ER. They had three wonderful children: Katy, Kara and Ken. Kelly lectured on surgical procedures, which involved traveling to medical facilities around the country. Because of a dream and her fear that she would one day be in an airplane accident, she drove her car, traveled by train and even took a boat once. Family vacations were planned based on location, allowing extra time to reach their destination via ground or by sea.

One winter morning, after enjoying breakfast with her family, Kelly left to attend one of her lectures. The road conditions were not favorable, but Kelly refused to fly with the rest of the surgical team, so she ventured out slowly through the snow. This was a very important lecture for the surgical team and the hospital and Kelly knew she must get there. As she was driving, sleet began to mix in with the heavy, falling snow. Suddenly, a large truck slid off the highway while Kelly's car and at least nine others collided. Fortunately, there were no fatal injuries. Ironically, the truck was carrying aircraft parts, which brought closure to Kelly's thoughts of being in an airplane accident.

Kelly's husband reminded her that flying is considered to be one of the safest forms of transportation. Kelly read the statistics presented by the Department of Transportation concluding that airline travel is twenty-nine times safer than driving an automobile. Statistics have little value to a fearful flyer; however, a realistic approach to overcoming fear does have value. Kelly realized that sitting around worrying about the dangers of flying made no sense. Kelly, like many fearful flyers, blamed her fear on the fact that life is vulnerable and that no one has full control over it, whether one travels by ground, rail, sea or air.

After her accident, Kelly realized that it was time to make changes. She worked on her fear of flying, stayed in the present and used my techniques and exercises to overcome her flight anxiety. Not only did she become a successful flyer, but also her family has enjoyed some really neat places and the hospital and surgical team couldn't be happier. Kelly realized she had to stop living in the "What Ifs?" She learned to be psychologically in control of her thoughts and feelings.

According to the National Institute of Mental Health, specific phobias like the fear of flying affect an estimated 19.2 million adult Americans and are twice as common in women as in men. If one can easily avoid the feared situations or the feared object, then one will not find help. When the avoidance interferes with one's personal life or career, it can become disabling and the fearful person will then usually seek help.

Do You Live in the "What Ifs?"

Just imagine if every time you got into your car you asked yourself, "What if the brakes give out? What if a truck hits me? What if the gas line blows up?" Or if every time it rains you ask yourself, "What if I get struck by lightning? What if a flood takes my house away? What if I go out and catch pneumonia? What if I go out and drown?" *What if…? What if...? What if...?* There is so much life has to offer. Grab onto it and enjoy every day as much as you possibly can. There is so much that you can miss if your fear handicaps you from experiencing life. Forget the "What Ifs?" and remember, "I can and I will!"

Before you begin the steps to free yourself of your fear of flying, refer to chapter 20 and take the **SUDS Test** on page 205. This will assess what aspects of flying you fear most and what you need to work on. At the end of the book, you should retake the test. Your goal is to lower your score from your first test so you can fly fear free.

What Is Fear?

Your fear is real. But fear is nothing more than fear of fear. Some argue it is a cognitive disorder; some argue it is a biological disorder. Several parts of the brain play a role in the production of anxiety and fear. Through brain imaging technology and neurochemical techniques, scientists have discovered that the *amygdala* and the *hippocampus* are key factors in most anxiety disorders. The amygdala, an almond-shaped structure embedded deep in the brain, is thought to be the communications center between the sections of the brain which process the incoming sensory signals and the sections which interpret these signals. It may alert the rest of the brain that a threat is present and then trigger anxiety or a fear response.[1]

To successfully eliminate your fear, you must define and understand it. It helps to have a psychological understanding of fear. Many of my clients appreciate the educational information you will read next. Do not become overwhelmed; it is here to help you clarify any thoughts or questions you may have regarding the etiology (causes) of fear.

Individuals with the fear of flying usually meet the criteria listed in the *Diagnostic and Statistical Manual of Mental Disorders IV-TR* for a Specific Phobia, Situational Type where the "situational type," or fear trigger, is air travel. The *DSM IV-TR* defines Specific Phobia, Situational Type as:

> If the fear is cued by a specific situation such as public transportation, tunnels, bridges, elevators, flying, driving or enclosed places. This subtype has a bimodal age-at-onset distribution, with one peak in childhood and another in the mid-20s.

The *DSM IV-TR* criteria for Agoraphobia state:

> Anxiety about being in places or situations from which escape might be difficult (or embarrassing) or in which help may not be available in the event of having an unexpected or predisposed panic attack or panic-like symptoms. Agoraphobic fears typically involve characteristic clusters of situations that include being outside the home alone; being in a crowd or standing in a line; being on a bridge; and traveling in a bus, train or automobile.

The *DSM IV-TR* criteria for Panic Disorder With Agoraphobia reveal:

> Sufferers must exhibit both (1) and (2) to be diagnosed:
> (1) Recurrent, unexpected panic attacks.
> (2) At least one of the attacks has been followed by one month (or more) of the following:
> a. Persistent concern about having additional attacks
> b. Worry about the implications of the attack or its consequences (e.g. losing control, having a heart attack, "going crazy")
> c. A significant change in behavior related to the attacks

Anticipatory Anxiety, or "Fear of Fear," begins with automatic, fearful thoughts such as *I'll die if I fly*. In brief, you begin to worry.[2] Many individuals fear particular situations that remind them of a traumatic experience, such as an earthquake. Sufferers can't go back into their homes, they have to sleep with their bedroom doors open and they are unable to take showers. They lose control of their lives.[3] This population lives in constant worry.

Fear of the Unknown is a very common term used in treating the fear of flying. Many who have never been on a plane do not know what to expect. After a traumatic experience or event like 9/11, people may feel more worried and fearful than normal. This is particularly true with unpredictable events. Experts in the field of aerophobia have found it helpful for fearful individuals to clarify what exactly it is they fear will happen when they fly. Three main factors which feed the fear are *anticipation, avoidance* and *fighting the fear*.[4] With *anticipation,* the fearful flyer will experience much anxiety prior to a flight. He or she experiences "what if" or hypothetical worry when he or she thinks of flying or even views a plane. The individual must discharge the negative influence of the anticipation to overcome the fear of flying. In *avoidance,* the stronger an individual's feelings about air travel, the more he or she will avoid flying or fly only if necessary. *Avoidance* can be addictive; it can be viewed as a reward as in Pavlov's *classical conditioning*.

Classical conditioning is a reflexive or natural response to a learned stimulus that indicates some internal or external event. There are four elements of classical conditioning: An *unconditioned stimulus* is something unlearned that happens in the brain which produces a response (e.g., avoiding or cancelling the flight). An *unconditioned response* is a natural, reflex behavior which does not have to be learned or taught (e.g., relief from the avoidance or cancellation of the flight). A *conditioned stimulus* is something which produces a response following learning (e.g., the suggestion of flying). A *conditioned response* is a behavior that is learned by the association made between the conditioned stimulus and an unconditioned stimulus (e.g., avoidance in response to the suggestion of flying).[5]

Fighting the Fear is the battle that fearful flyers have to manage so that they can fly. Many of these people are "white knuckle" flyers, holding on for dear life while in-flight. Some self-medicate with drugs or alcohol. According to a study by Frank Wilhelm and Walton Roth of the Stanford University School of Medicine, more than 60 percent of fearful fliers have used sedatives or alcohol to try to reduce their fear.[6]

Jerilyn Ross, president of the Anxiety Disorders Association of America, claims that alcohol may serve as a temporary relaxant for fearful fliers but that it also makes them anxious and interferes with their ability to work after landing. A prescribed medication may relax a fearful flier who occasionally flies, but it is not the answer for long-term treatment of the problem.[7]

Jenny's Story

"I'm scared to death of flying. I used to fly, but now I can't get myself even close to an airport. Just the thought of seeing a plane makes me sick. It's a dreadful feeling when that airplane door closes, and the fasten seat belt sign is illuminated. I feel trapped. My heart pounds and my hands sweat. If somebody starts talking to me, I get very nervous and preoccupied with my fearful thoughts. When the captain makes the announcement that we have been cleared for take-off, I feel sick to my stomach. As the airplane starts to ascend, it just reinforces that feeling that I can't get out. I see myself losing control, jumping out of my seat, running down the aisle to the door, but of course it never happens. I'm not afraid of closed spaces or heights, but I'm deathly afraid of flying. I'm afraid of dying in a plane crash. Whenever I've thought about a career change, I've had to ask myself, *Will I be required to fly?* I only go places where I can drive, take a train or even a bus. My family and friends draw attention to the fact that I couldn't get off a train traveling at excessive speeds either, so why don't trains bother me? I just tell them it isn't a rational fear and that I have my reasons."

WHY ARE *YOU* AFRAID TO FLY?

Circle either "Yes" or "No" to complete this list of questions. Those that you answer "Yes" to point out the possible causes of your fear, so you can think more rationally, work on your problem and overcome your fear. Remember, "I can and I will!"

1.	Yes	No	I don't like being in closed spaces. I feel trapped and fearful that I can't get out.
2.	Yes	No	If I fly, I know the plane will crash and I will die.
3.	Yes	No	I have a fear of being around people or away from my home.
4.	Yes	No	I have a fear of heights and don't like being up in the sky.
5.	Yes	No	I'm afraid of panicking and losing control on the plane.
6.	Yes	No	I don't have an understanding of the airplane, the flight crew or the airline industry.
7.	Yes	No	I'm afraid of another terrorist attack.
8.	Yes	No	On my last flight, I experienced terrible turbulence and thought we were falling.
9.	Yes	No	I have asthma and I'm afraid of having an in-flight attack.
10.	Yes	No	I don't like people. I get very nervous around large crowds of people.
11.	Yes	No	I'm afraid that there might be an earthquake or a tsunami and we won't land.
12.	Yes	No	I had a dream that I was in a plane crash and I'm afraid to fly.
13.	Yes	No	I like to be in the driver's seat, so that I can make sure everything is okay.

Causes

1. Claustrophobia
2. Aviophobia/Aerophobia: Fearful that the plane is going to crash
3. Agoraphobia: Fearful of being around people or away from home
4. Acrophobia: Fearful of heights
5. Panic attacks: Fearful of losing control and experiencing a panic attack
6. Fear of the unknown
7. Fear of terrorists
8. Bad flying experience
9. Illness
10. Social phobia
11. Natural disasters
12. Superstition or premonition
13. Fear of giving up control

Seven Steps to More Comfortable Air Travel

Here are seven steps to flying more comfortably. As we move on in the next chapters of this book, you will be given additional techniques to help conquer your fear of flying, but refer back to these steps as you progress.

Step 1: Gain knowledge of and trust in the airline industry.

Step 2: Use positive self-talk and motivation.

Step 3: Use relaxation exercises.

Step 4: Use breathing exercises.

Step 5: Use supportive items while on the plane (e.g., books, CDs, comics, pictures, colors).

Step 6: Use a thought-stopping process (rubber band on hand) to break the "What Ifs?"

Step 7: Use visualization exercises (e.g., guided imagery).

Points to Remember

You've started on an exciting journey toward a successful flight with many flights to follow. The key to fear-free air travel is to stay motivated, positive and in control of your thoughts. Use the exercises and techniques, be willing to make changes and believe that "I can and I will!"

Fear of flying is real, but you can work to overcome your fear and have fun doing so. Specific phobias like the fear of flying (aerophobia) affect millions of people worldwide; you are not alone. Forget the "What Ifs?" To successfully eliminate the problem, you must define and understand it. You should practice using the techniques, exercises and the Seven Steps to More Comfortable Air Travel to help fly free of fear.

Key Questions

1. Why are you afraid to fly?
2. What will be your first steps to overcoming your fear?
3. What items can you use to relieve stress and relax during the process of overcoming your fear?

chapter 2

Answers to Common Questions

chapter goals:

To address fear of flying statistics and to answer the questions that you and many fearful flyers have.

To help you realize that you are not alone in this fear.

It's easy to feel like you're the only person who is afraid of flying. But one out of every six Americans and millions more around the world suffer from aerophobia. And due to their fear of flying and anxiety, some avoid flying altogether. Recent surveys suggest that 27 percent of American adults are somewhat fearful of flying and that 9 percent are "very afraid." Shortly after 9/11, one poll indicated that 43 percent were somewhat concerned about getting on an airplane and 17 percent were "very afraid."

The Boeing Company, which is one of the largest aircraft manufacturers in the world, estimates that over twenty-five million adults in the United States experience various levels of flight anxiety. Around two billion passengers board the world's airlines every year and many of these travelers fly out of necessity.

Air Travel Is Safe

Statistics show that air travel is one of the safest types of transportation, although many who are afraid to fly have trouble believing that.

In 2008, 34,017 Americans died in automobile-related accidents, but between 1982 and 2010 only 3,288 Americans died from airline-related accidents, which means it would take over 117 years of airline deaths to equal the number of auto-related fatalities that occurred just in 2008. Calculating the deaths per 100 million miles traveled in the United States, an American is 190 times more likely to die in an auto accident versus an airline accident.[1]

So why do people concentrate on airline-related deaths versus those caused by other means of transportation? The media tend to focus on any airline crash anywhere in the world. They report on crowded airports, flight delays, cancellations, weather, small aircraft accidents, a near miss, etc. But how many times do you hear about someone getting a flat tire on their car or being delayed to pick up a child at school due to the weather? Oversaturated media coverage gives the public the idea that airlines are unsafe. The repeated negative information can be stressful, not only for a fearful flyer, but also for most of the viewers. If something negative related to air travel comes on, change the channel or turn off the radio or television. Don't listen to the repeated details. There is an average of about ninety people who die per day in car-related accidents; this is diffused during the course of the day and throughout the world. But even though airline accidents are rare, hearing about hundreds of people dying at one time in an airline accident resonates with you.

Airline transportation safety, compared to all other means of travel, is far superior. Our security and safety process has only improved since 9/11. However, feelings of fear can come from fear itself. Fear is not usually from the danger, but from the dreadful anticipations and automatic thoughts of a possibly disastrous event. If you stop normal activities and behavior because of your fear, then you have given in to it. Don't let fear take hold of you.

What Is My Problem?

You don't have to hide when people talk about flying. Many who take air travel are not comfortable flyers. Only 6 percent of the people who fly are completely comfortable about flying. Keep in mind, fear of flying is curable with motivation, positive thinking and time put into working on your fear. Many fearful flyers have stopped flying because of the despair they feel that nothing has worked to free them of their fear.

People who suffer from flight fear are generally intelligent, successful, perfectionist, caring, artistic, creative, business-oriented and conscientious. There is a diverse mix of fearful flyers that consists of various occupations, races, cultures, genders and ages around the world.

One of the reasons the average person might not be comfortable about using air travel is because it is not a frequent occurrence, but celebrities travel by plane much more often and still admit they are uncomfortable and nervous about flying. Some public figures who have openly disclosed that they are fearful flyers include Jennifer Aniston, Oprah Winfrey, Whoopi Goldberg, Ronald Reagan, Megan Fox, Aretha Franklin and John Madden among many others. In fact, it was reported that the reason NFL defensive star and Super Bowl XLIII champion James Harrison wouldn't meet with President Obama at the White House was because he has a fear of flying.

My own clinical findings support that there is not just one but many causes of flight fear and so the best treatment requires an eclectic and holistic approach. A fearful flyer who suffers with panic disorder usually has more than one fearful stimulus. Regardless of the cause of one's fear of flying, I advocate an eclectic-holistic approach for treating fear of flying and for meeting individual needs. This book employs that approach.

Getting Help for Flight Fear

You have already helped yourself by using this self-help book! Several studies conclude that the fear of flying can be lessened by multicomponent treatments such as self-help books, DVDs and hypnosis. For more severe cases, virtual reality has been found to be effective; Virtual Reality Therapy (VRT) or Virtual Reality Graded Exposure Therapy (VRGET) is a type of Cognitive-Behavioral Therapy (CBT) intervention that uses computer-generated images for flight fear. It has proven successful and more cost-effective than taking a real flight In Vivo Exposure (IVE). CBT is a type of psychotherapy which lessens destructive emotions by correcting negative thoughts and encouraging healthy mental exercises. This involves exposure therapy, cognitive restructuring and relaxation techniques. CBT has been found by professionals, private programs and airline programs to be effective and cost-efficient for panic disorder and fear of flying. *Exposure therapy* forces the individual to face what they fear. The goal is *habituation,* a type of learning where response to stimulus diminishes with repeated contact.

The National Institute of Mental Health supports that successful treatment is usually CBT, which is included in this self-help book. VRGET and virtual treatments are effective for treating fear of flying and other phobias, but one study showed that there are disadvantages to their use for those who experience transient symptoms of disorientation, nausea, dizziness, headache and blurred vision while in a virtual environment. Many are uncomfortable wearing the headgear or looking into the device for a lengthy period of time. Also, VRGET has been found to trigger migraines, seizures or gait abnormalities in those individuals who are prone to these medical conditions. Those individuals who have disorders of the vestibular system and those patients with psychosis should not use VRGET.[2]

Although CBT has been the most utilized treatment modality, a *multimodal treatment,* which is a combination of various models, may be effective in the treatment of flight fear. Multimodal treatment is becoming more effective, because it meets individuals' needs. Psychologists and other practitioners find that many individuals do not respond well to traditional therapies or those frequently practiced in a program or by a specialty therapist or doctor. Along with the different theories, models and techniques, therapists are finding that alternative therapies are very effective for many sufferers of the fear of flying as well as other disorders and illnesses. Alternative therapies found to be helpful for individuals with the fear of flying or other disorders include Music Therapy, Aromatherapy, Guided Imagery, Progressive Muscle Relaxation, Hypnosis, and Meditation. You will learn these techniques in this book.

Most drug therapy efforts have been unsuccessful in treating flight fear. Passengers often medicate with sedatives, including benzodiazepines and alcohol, but these typically only provide short-term relief.

Follow the material provided in this book, use the exercises and techniques and stay motivated with a positive attitude.

In chapter 22 we will discuss what to do when self-help is not enough. So, for now, you are on the right track to success!

Attending Seminars and Individual Sessions

As the number of air travelers has grown worldwide, interest in anxiety associated with flying also has grown. There has been an increase in programs around the world including those run by airlines, private persons or mental health professionals for treating individuals who suffer from flight fear.

Helpful Seminars

There are several individuals, professionals and businesses including airlines who conduct seminars and workshops. These programs may provide help, but they can be costly.

Fear of Flying Clinics

As the facilitator and psychotherapist at a clinic for fearful flyers, I lead a discussion about the fear of flying and teach attendees about their fear. I give a lecture on the airline industry with questions and answers from the audience. In the clinic, aircraft are described and various helpful tips for pleasant flying are discussed. Intervention through relaxation techniques, deep breathing and other exercises is taught, processed and practiced, focusing on reality, not the hypothetical fear. Cognitive-Behavioral Therapy with an eclectic approach is utilized. Attendees are given an audio simulation of a flight and the procedures from arrival at the airport to landing are discussed. They are given information on how to create a personalized flight plan. Coping strategies for anticipatory anxiety are practiced. Safety and security information is discussed and processed along with concerns. The simulation flight is optional as needed. Videos and biblio-therapy are used for visualization exercises and education. Individual sessions are recommended for those who need further assistance in working on their flight fear. My seminar costs approximately three hundred dollars and takes place on the weekend. Many seminars follow a similar format.

Individual Sessions

There are many professionals who offer individual sessions for the fear of flying, including psychologists, psychotherapists, psychiatrists, counselors, clinical social workers, pilots, etc. A fifty-minute session can cost from sixty to three hundred dollars.

There are a few fearful flyers who may need a more clinical approach. If you are what I classify as a "Level Nine or Level Ten Fearful Flyer" (unable to let go and take control of your fear or unaware and/or in denial of an underlying problem), you can still successfully overcome your flight fear by following my program for *Systematic Desensitization.* But it is important to continue using the techniques and exercises in this book.

Telephone Consultation

Telephone counseling is beneficial for individuals who live in rural areas and/or do not have access to a therapist. It is also beneficial for those with medical conditions or those who suffer from agoraphobia. It is available to and convenient for those who cannot leave their homes.

Why Do Plane Crashes Happen?

Accidents happen. Fortunately, we do not see many in the airline industry. But there have indeed been accidents and many of you ask, "Why?" Upon reviewing past incidents, here are a few causes of airplane accidents:

- Design flaws
- Faulty maintenance
- Structural failure
- Structural fatigue
- Human error
- Weather conditions
- Natural causes (e.g., birds flying into the plane's engine)

You may have heard of the airplane's black box. After being salvaged from an airplane accident, it usually reveals the cause of the accident to aviation investigators.

Lorenda Ward, a leading aviation crash investigator for the National Transportation Safety Board (NTSB), chooses to focus on air travel safety rather than airline tragedies. Ward believes the findings from airplane accidents, which result in new FAA guidelines, help prevent repeated disasters. After seeing the worst in airplane travel, she continues to enjoy flying just as she always has.[3] The FAA and the NTSB's investigations, inspections, guidelines and rules constantly improve air travel safety.

Even though you hear saturated media coverage on airline incidents, like when a Southwest Airlines 737 had a rip in its metal frame, what you may not have heard was that eighty Southwest planes were grounded for inspection to ensure their safety. Mechanics check each plane before every flight. Do you have your car checked every time you drive it?

Remember, an airplane incident is news and it is the media's job to tell it. Everyone loves to hear a good story, especially when it is about something big like an airline accident. If it bothers you, just turn it off. It does not help to keep listening to or watching a subject that you find upsetting.

RATE YOUR LEVEL OF ANXIETY

Relax. As you think of or visualize a trigger (security, takeoff, landing, turbulence, etc.), rate it.

LEVEL 1: No Anxiety
LEVEL 2: Extremely Low Anxiety
LEVEL 3: Somewhat Low Anxiety
LEVEL 4: Low Anxiety
LEVEL 5: Medium Low Anxiety
LEVEL 6: Medium Anxiety
LEVEL 7: Medium High Anxiety
LEVEL 8: High Anxiety
LEVEL 9: Extremely High Anxiety
LEVEL 10: Uncontrollable Anxiety

Points to Remember

You are not alone; millions of people are afraid to fly. Flying is considered one hundred times safer than driving a car. The nature of the problem varies for each individual. To successfully eliminate fear you must define and understand your problem. You can get started by using this self-help book. If you require additional assistance, you may find group seminars or individual sessions helpful. It can be costly. The length of time for seminars and individual sessions varies by the program's design and your individual needs. Everything that you will find in most seminars you have right here in this book.

Key Questions

1. How dangerous is flying on an airplane?
2. What is the nature of your fear of flying?
3. How will you get help for fear of flying?

chapter 3

Causes of Your Flight Fear

chapter goals:

To address the causes of your problem by explaining panic attacks, anxiety, claustrophobia, acrophobia, aerophobia and unknown fear.

To help you discover what may be causing your fear so that you can successfully make changes to rid yourself of the fear.

Before you can overcome your fear of flying, it helps to determine the cause of your fear and to understand the problem. To eliminate fear, we will use a behavioral approach, which focuses on the present and employs helpful exercises and techniques. It is time to better understand your fear, so let's move forward.

Defining and Understanding Your Anxiety

Many who experience fear of flying are among those who suffer from aerophobia (fear of flying), acrophobia (fear of heights), claustrophobia (fear of enclosed spaces) and agoraphobia (fear of having a panic attack and not being able to escape or get help). You may also fear air travel because you don't have accurate information about air travel. Or you may suffer from Post Traumatic Stress Disorder (PTSD) after experiencing an uncomfortable flight in your past.

Studies conducted on the fear of flying in various countries indicate that the mean age of the sufferers is around the late thirties to early forties and predominantly women. Results indicate that the frequent use of alcohol and sedatives in-flight suggests a larger "subthreshold" of flight fear in the general population. The increase in flight anxiety could be due to the increased airport security due to terrorist attacks.[1] Researchers debate whether or not the media stresses the population by reporting airport crowds, flight delays, cancellations, weather, small aircraft accidents or near misses which can then lead to work-related stress or air travel avoidance.[2] Individuals can have a genetic or biological factor which causes the fear.

What is Aviophobia or Aerophobia?

Aviophobia/Aerophobia is the fear that the plane is going to crash.

Aviophobia affects 10 to 50 percent of the population. Aerophobia presents with a high level of anxiety. An individual may refuse to take air travel or find it tremendously stressful. Most who suffer from flight anxiety have flown for years before becoming afraid, while some individuals have been fearful of flying all their lives.[3]

Remember Kelly, the surgeon, who had the fear of being killed in an airplane accident? Also Jenny, who was afraid of dying in a plane crash? Both suffered from aviophobia. Now here are Carrie's and Lauren's stories. I treated Carrie for her aviophobia over four sessions and I met with Lauren for eight sessions.

Carrie's Fear

Carrie is a thirteen-year-old female in excellent health. Her personality is pleasant and she appears happy and very well-mannered. She is an only child and has a very close family network. Her social circle consists of her family, school friends and her dog. She has never worked and appears to be quite intelligent. For a child, she is exceptionally self-confident and has a positive attitude toward life. She believes others view her positively.

Carrie wants to fly without fear. She is afraid that the plane is going to crash. She didn't like the sounds she heard when she flew to California for a family vacation a few years prior. She also suffered from ear pain on the flight. Carrie is also experiencing nightmares wherein the airplane on which she is travelling crashes.

Carrie's goals in treatment are to learn about the sounds of the plane, to eliminate her nightmares about flying and to learn a method she can employ on the airplane to stop ear pain. Carrie hopes to get past her fears before a trip to Europe with her parents.

Treatment: Carrie learned about aircraft mechanisms, procedures and safety and also learned relaxation exercises. In our therapeutic discussions, Carrie expressed concern about dying and leaving her family—a concern that was alleviated in subsequent discussion. Carrie also learned a technique to eliminate ear discomfort during air travel. Lastly, Carrie was given five steps to make positive changes regarding her nightmares.

Results: Carrie experienced a successful flight soon after treatment using the tools she gained in therapy. She now understands the sounds of the airplane, no longer experiences nightmares and makes sure to ask the flight attendant for warm, moist paper napkins and a cup to eliminate ear pain (you will learn this technique later in the book). She looks forward to a second flight to Europe in the near future and claims her aerophobia is extinct.

Lauren's Fear

Lauren is a fifty-year-old female in good health who has had some medical concerns in her past. She appears happy, caring, outgoing and self-confident. She is very religious. She has a large, close-knit family. Lauren and her husband attend many social events, though most of her relationships are with church members and social groups. Lauren is well-educated and attends graduate school, where she studies English and teaches religion. She has experienced migraine headaches on multiple occasions. She believes that others view her as quiet, aloof, religious and financially secure.

Lauren wants to end her "automatic catastrophic thoughts" about air travel. The thought of flying in an airplane produces automatic visions of disastrous events like crashing or a hijacking. These thoughts were exacerbated by 9/11.

Lauren's goal in treatment is to learn some methods that can help her feel more at ease with air travel.

Treatment: Although she had flown numerous times, Lauren disclosed an underlying fear of crashing due to a lack of faith in the security system. So she learned about the ongoing training and qualifications of the flight crew and about the continual monitoring of security procedures at airport checkpoints. Lauren learned relaxation techniques and was referred to a physician to alleviate her migraine headaches. A holistic approach to treatment that employed meditation, spirituality and music was implemented.

Results: Lauren was comforted by the knowledge she gained about the safety of the airline industry. She now uses her relaxation techniques, such as guided imagery (about which you will learn later in this book), meditation and prayer. She has made several airplane trips with her family since therapy.

Understanding Panic Attacks

Panic Attacks are intense periods of anxiety that can be triggered by air travel. Panic disorder affects 3.5 percent of the population throughout a lifetime; the statistics show that it affects twice as many women as men, and it usually presents with depression and other anxiety disorders.[4] The *Diagnostic and Statistical Manual of Mental Disorders IV-TR* defines panic attacks as:

> Discrete periods of intense fear or discomfort in which four or more of the following symptoms are found: palpitations, pounding heart, increased heart rate, sweating, trembling, shaking, sensations of shortness of breath or smothering, feeling of choking, chest pain or discomfort, nausea or abdominal distress, feeling dizzy, unsteady, light-headed or faint, de-realization, depersonalization, fear of losing control or going crazy, fear of dying, numbness or tingling, chills or hot flushes. These symptoms occur abruptly and reach a peak within ten minutes. Panic attacks may occur in many anxiety disorders, for instance on exposure to the feared object in specific phobia, the fear-provoking memory in PTSD, or the obsessive thought in OCD, and are not in and of themselves considered an anxiety disorder.

Panic disorder involves a sudden, intense and unprovoked feeling of terror and dread. Individuals who suffer from this disorder generally develop strong fears about when and where their next panic attacks will occur, often restricting their activities as a result.

Panic attacks frequently occur with *agoraphobia,* which is the fear of being in places or situations from which escape might be difficult or where help is unavailable if a symptom were to develop that caused embarrassment. Individuals who suffer from agoraphobia have a fear of leaving a familiar home setting; they fear open spaces, parking lots, grocery stores, malls, arenas, crossing a bridge or traveling by public transportation, especially airplanes. Symptoms experienced by agoraphobic individuals include dizziness or falling, heart palpitations, tachycardia, chest pain, loss of bladder or bowel control, nausea, vomiting and difficulty breathing. Agoraphobia can cause an individual to restrict his or her travel or require a companion to accompany him or her when away from his or her safe place, which is usually home.

Panic attacks are focused more on the individual's self than the airplane. They are caused by a combination of psychological and biological reactions overstressing the body. *Thought stopping* and *relaxation exercises* (which will be discussed later) have been very successful in dealing with this fear. Those suffering panic attacks should remain focused and realize that they are not in any real danger. With treatment and practice, people who suffer from anxiety or panic disorders can live normal lives.

Understanding Claustrophobia

Claustrophobia is the fear of closed-in or tight spaces.

The majority of fearful fliers are afraid of having panic attacks on the plane due to claustrophobia.[5]

It's common for people who suffer from claustrophobia to expect to suffocate because of lack of oxygen as they walk down the jet bridge or board the plane. Their fear becomes a "self-fulfilling prophecy." The majority of the time there is no existing danger; however, sufferers of aviophobia perceive there is and their anxiety may occur from the *fight-or-flight* reaction or *acute stress.* As an animal faces possible danger, there is a heightened alertness that results in several physical changes in the body, like tachycardia (rapid breathing) and constriction or dilation of blood vessels.

If you suffer from claustrophobia, there are several exercises you can use to help overcome your fear. Color therapy, relaxation and breathing exercises have been very successful in dealing with this fear.

I treated Joe over eight sessions for his claustrophobia and flight fear. Here is his case:

Joe's Fears

Joe is a twenty-eight-year-old male in excellent health. He appears confident and well-mannered with an outgoing personality. He is an only child and was raised by his father. His mother died when he was five years old. His social circle consists of his friends, teammates and cousins. He completed college on a basketball scholarship and has been playing for a professional team for five years. He believes others view him with admiration and that people generally find him to be a strong athlete, a joker, financially secure, a role model and a loyal friend.

Joe wants to get over his fear of air travel. As a professional basketball player, he has travelled by air often. After 9/11 and recent air travel incidents, Joe's resolve has wavered. He is embarrassed about his fear, because he is seen as a "big guy." Joe feels claustrophobic when on a plane and on his most recent flight he nearly exited the plane prior to takeoff.

Joe's goals for treatment are to eliminate his fear of air travel and not to be embarrassed. He wants quick and simple techniques that he can use to make air travel more comfortable. Joe wants to feel in control of turbulence and his experience on the flight.

Treatment: Joe disclosed in therapy that a friend had died in a plane crash. This contributed to his claustrophobia and his concerns were alleviated in subsequent sessions. Joe learned to employ guided imagery, breathing exercises and a holistic approach to fear relief (color therapy, music therapy and dream therapy).

Results: Joe's claustrophobia and aviophobia are nearly eliminated. On a flight directly following treatment, he used the stress-reducing techniques and exercises that he had learned and practiced. Joe claims the information he learned about the airline industry and the quick, effective techniques he used were primary reasons for his success.

Understanding Acrophobia

Acrophobia is the fear of heights.

Not only are some individuals with the fear of flying worried and fearful of the flight, but also their underlying origin of fear can be due to *acrophobia*. Countless individuals are afraid of heights, not of flying.

One psychiatrist with whom I am associated disclosed his own embarrassment at having "such a phobia" and explaining how individuals suffering with fear have to face not only the fear, but also the embarrassment that often accompanies it. From the words of an acrophobic and professional:

> "I felt waves of vertigo, anxiety and deep, deep embarrassment…Yet there I was, paralyzed. It was so utterly weird that these people and I were seeing the same world, the same situation, and yet for me, it was paralyzing, while for others it held interest, beauty, wonder…"[6]

Individuals who suffer from acrophobia experience anxiety and dizziness when they are exposed to heights. One possible cause of this problem is that the sufferer's balance system is disturbed, although studies suggest that height overestimation may be caused by fear.[7]

It appears that as we become older and wiser, many of us become more fearful of heights. Also, if there was something in your past which frightened you, such as being pushed or falling from a high place, you could experience the fear of heights. If you suffer from *acrophobia,* uncovering incidents from your past could be important in the treatment of your fear of heights.

I treated Teri, a young woman with acrophobia and aviophobia, over eight sessions. Here is her story:

Teri's Fears

Teri is a twenty-one-year-old female in excellent health. She appears pleasant, self-confident, motivated, outgoing and slightly anxious. She is the oldest child of three. She is a college senior who lives off-campus with three other students. Teri is a musician and wants to cure her fear of flying before joining a travelling symphony orchestra to which she has been accepted.

She is afraid of heights and thinks that the plane might fall from the sky during flight. An apprehensive person, Teri can't seem to figure out how an airplane could continue to fly if one or all of the engines stopped running.

Teri's goals for treatment are to stop worrying about the plane falling out of the sky and to get over her fear of heights. She wants to be able to enjoy her orchestra's concerts without worrying about transportation.

Treatment: Teri learned about the air travel industry, procedures and safety. For her acrophobia, Teri was desensitized to height using a cognitive-behavioral approach in treatment and the fear diminished greatly.

Result: Teri now enjoys air travel and says her acrophobia is completely eliminated—whether she is on an airplane or not.

Fear of the Unknown

Fear of the Unknown is, in terms of air travel, the fear of not having an understanding of the airplane, flight crew or airline industry.

Fear of the unknown is a very common term used in fear of flying. Many who have never been on a plane do not know what to expect. There is a storm of misinformation about airplanes, pilots and the airline industry.[8] You will learn all the aspects of air travel in this book so that you can conquer the fear of the unknown.

WHY ARE *YOU* AFRAID TO FLY?

This exercise lists the main reasons that cause individuals to be afraid to fly. After reading each possible cause of the fear of flying, give a rating score from one to five, to determine how much each cause contributes to your uncomfortable feelings or flight fear.

Completing this exercise will help you in several ways. First, you can discover the underlying problem that is causing your fear of flying. Second, you'll realize that thousands of other people experience the same problem. Third, you'll have a better understanding about what's causing your fear. Rate each potential cause of the fear from one to five: (1) no problem, (2) somewhat fearful, (3) moderately fearful, (4) extremely fearful or (5) close to panic. You'll discover the problem you are having the most difficulty overcoming. After this exercise, you can decide which cause(s) of the problem you want to work on first.

________ Aviophobia/Aerophobia

________ Panic Attacks

_______ Agoraphobia

_______ Claustrophobia

_______ Acrophobia

_______ Fear of the Unknown

_______ Other (Please write down and work through)

____

____

____

Points to Remember

Some individuals have never heard of the words *aviophobia* or *aerophobia.* People who suffer from this are people who are positive that if they do fly, the plane is going to crash and that they will die.

Panic attack is a dramatic attack of fear with physical symptoms. These attacks mimic the body's physiological response to a life-threatening situation. Panic attacks are sudden and unpredictable.

Claustrophobia is the fear of closed spaces, not just airplanes, and sufferers are more comfortable in large planes rather than small ones. The jet bridge or jet way to the plane, which can get crowded, can present a barrier to people who are afraid they will be trapped in a small space and not be able to breathe. That is a common reaction for people who have any number of phobias and for those who have anxiety attacks.

Acrophobia is the fear of heights. For many individuals who suffer from acrophobia, flying at 34,000 feet raises their anxiety level, and being at that height results in feelings of terror, particularly when the plane shakes or bounces as it often does in turbulence.

Fear of the unknown is common among individuals who have never flown on a plane. They do not understand the airline industry, aircraft dynamics, the flight crew's training, the plane's sounds and its movement. Most individuals who fall into this class love to travel by air once they take their first flight.

To fly comfortably and without fear, it helps to discover and understand your fear and work conscientiously on your problem with a positive and open mind.

Key Questions

1. Can you define and understand your problem?
2. What steps will you take to address your phobia?
3. Assess your confidence and anxiety level at this stage of your self-help therapy.

chapter 4

Seven Common Worries

chapter goals:

To address the seven worries that commonly afflict those individuals who suffer from flight fear.

To answer questions about birds, thunderstorms, tsunamis, turbulence, takeoff, landing and terrorist attacks.

Fearful flyers most commonly have worries about wild birds, thunderstorms, tsunamis, turbulence, takeoff and landing conditions or terrorists. In this chapter, we'll discuss the validity of those concerns but recognize the improbability of their occurrence. Regardless of the concern, remember that the crew and others involved in the safety of your flight are well trained to handle the plane and any situation it may encounter.

How Can Birds Threaten Safety?

When Captain Chesley Burnett Sullenberger III, pilot of US Airways Flight 1549, skillfully and safely landed a plane in the Hudson River, people were alerted to the problem birds pose to flight safety. Because of this incident and those similar to it, birds have become a concern for the FAA and the airlines. Planes' engines will not be affected by being struck by birds under four pounds and pilots are trained to handle bird-related incidents. Certain airports, especially those along coastal areas, use border collies, scarecrows, horns, whistles, bells and shotguns to keep bird strikes from interfering with aircraft safety.

How Can Thunderstorms Threaten Safety?

Pilots and air traffic controllers work together to keep your plane away from rough weather, but airplanes are designed and built to withstand all weather conditions. There are exceptions in extreme situations, like when a tornado went through St. Louis, causing extensive damage to Lambert International Airport in April 2011. The tornado moved a few jumbo jets twenty yards and the airport was shut down. The airport immediately went under generator power while 80,000 people were without power in St. Louis. Other than one concourse, the airport was fully operational within a few days. The weather is well-monitored and so you may see delays. Although most air travelers don't appreciate losing time, these delays are for their safety.

Thunderstorms contribute to the turbulence you may experience in-flight. Working with the air traffic controllers, the pilot will try to fly around storms. Prior to departure, the flight crew studies weather charts to figure out the best altitude and location at which to fly. During the flight, the cockpit crew will look for signs of turbulence, such as rapid changes in atmospheric temperature, barometric pressure and wind speed or direction. The plane will remain on the ground if a thunderstorm is near the airport. If airborne, planes will stay a safe distance away from the destination airport until the storm moves out.

The plane's nose cone (or radome) can detect rain showers, thunderstorms and turbulence.

Lightning

Due to modern innovations, there is little chance of an airplane being struck by lightning, as planes are designed to channel strikes away from the aircraft. Although lightning frightens many passengers, strikes are highly unlikely and would probably not be damaging, as the electrical system is well insulated by surge protectors.

Hail

Pilots move quickly through hail, if they can't fly around it, and you may hear it hitting the outside of the plane. It can damage the paint and make a few dents, but it poses no real threat to the aircraft.

Tornados or Hurricanes

In the event of a tornado or hurricane, the weather is monitored by the flight crew and no aircraft will fly if the situation is dangerous. Flights will be cleared for landing or takeoff once the weather alert has been lifted. If the situation is extreme, the airplane will be rerouted to another airport.

Many fearful flyers are concerned about flying during storms, especially with recent increases in tornado activity. We can't stop Mother Nature, but taking precautions and being patient and prepared while following instructions can provide for your safety. Your aircraft will not be permitted to fly if there is any chance for danger.

Ice Problems

All airplanes have an anti-icing mechanism that is used in any icy condition. Anti-icing fluid is also applied to the wings as a matter of course. The plane's built-in engine and wing anti-icing will be employed to prevent ice buildup when operating near the freezing point and when observable moisture is present.

Should Tsunamis Be a Concern?

When a tsunami warning is issued, any aircraft would be rerouted to another airport if the destination airport is in danger. Flights would be cancelled and passengers would follow the safety procedures for a tsunami or earthquake. A tsunami warning must be taken seriously and one must act quickly to move to higher ground for safety. All rules for earthquakes should also be followed. In both situations, safety measures are respected and the situation is monitored.

Is Turbulence Dangerous?

Most fearful flyers admit that their greatest worry is turbulence. Though I often hear the question, "Can't the wings fall off?", wings are made to withstand severe turbulence. Aircraft are constructed to withstand extreme conditions beyond anything you would ever experience on a commercial flight and the airplanes are regularly inspected and maintained for your safety. The wings of an airplane are built strong and flexible to allow for turbulence.

Turbulence is caused by clouds, air masses, fronts and convection. Turbulence is elevated when a plane is around buildings and mountains (which alter wind conditions), deserts (uneven heating on the earth's surface) and rough air. Radar at night, along with visual ability during daylight, helps make it possible to travel around any extreme turbulence. It may feel like being on a roller-coaster ride, in a fast-moving elevator or in the backseat of a speeding car taking a curve.

One of the more common types of turbulence is caused by convective heating. As the sun warms the ground, the hot air rises and creates a bouncy feeling for passengers in an airplane. Evidence of this can be seen as small, puffy clouds. This type of turbulence is normally limited to lower altitudes. You might feel convective turbulence directly after takeoff or before landing on hot, sunny afternoons. It will cause you no danger and is categorized as light or mild turbulence.

Thunderstorms cause a mix of hot and cold air carrying a high volume of moisture to extremely high altitudes, resulting in turbulence. The air whips up and down, creating a thunderstorm. Thunderstorms can rise to 40,000 or 50,000 feet, creating some bumpy weather. If a storm is above 20,000 feet, the cockpit crew will fly up to twenty miles away to avoid any severe turbulence. The plane will also fly on the upwind side of the storm, avoiding hail and turbulence. Slowing the airspeed will help deliver a smoother ride.

Your experience of discomfort during in-flight turbulence is usually due to either downward acceleration of the plane, which causes a feeling of weightlessness, or upward acceleration of the plane, which causes a feeling of heaviness, both of which can make you feel uncomfortable at times. In severe turbulence, you may experience some nausea, dizziness, light-headedness and perspiration.

Your ears play a role in how you handle turbulence. The peripheral mechanism that first detects your changing motion in space over time (acceleration) contains two sets of three semi-circular canals which sit on top of the inner ears, one set for each ear. These are each connected to two sacs or vestibules, the *utricle* and the *saccule*, and each contains its own type of fluid.

Feelings During Turbulence

Psychologically, what you feel during turbulence is often associated with an innate fear of falling. At first, the airplane moves upward then levels off to cruising status and frequent flyers understand that soon a downward acceleration will occur. When you fly on an airplane, not only is your psyche aware that the airplane is flying above the ground, but also you associate coming down with falling. Use what you know about flying and the safety of airplanes (and what you know about physics) to put this fear into perspective and realize that you are safe.

Takeoff, Cruise and Landing

Understanding Takeoff

Takeoff can be one of the most nerve-racking parts of flying. What can you expect? After the plane taxies to its assigned runway and has been cleared for takeoff, the captain will announce, "Flight attendants, prepare for takeoff." Then the airplane will start rolling and move faster and faster down the runway until the nose of the plane tips upward. This is when you may hear noises that sound like rattling, thumping, drilling or high-pitched whining.

As the nose of the plane lifts, those sitting in the front of the plane will feel a rising sensation and passengers seated in the back will feel a falling sensation. You will also be pushed gently back in your seat by the acceleration. This is a good time to take your mind off the flight and use some of the techniques that you will learn in part III of this book.

In 1981, the FAA enacted regulations to help avoid accidents due to diverted attention. Commonly known as the "sterile cockpit rule," these regulations specifically prohibit crew member performance of non-essential duties or activities while the aircraft is involved in taxiing, takeoff, landing and all other flight operations conducted below 10,000 feet, except cruise flight. During the "sterile cockpit period," no one can enter the cockpit.

When a flight crew's attention is diverted from the task of flying, the chances for errors increase. Takeoff and landing are critical times for the flight. The flight crew may be setting the flaps prior to takeoff, extending the landing gear before landing, monitoring altitude on an instrument approach or using engine anti-ice for takeoff during a snow storm.

Shortly after takeoff you may hear noises as the landing gear is retracted. It won't take very long until the plane reaches 10,000 feet. You will hear a "ding" telling you that it is now safe to use electronic devices such as video games, audio devices, computers or video players. Other dings you will hear are passengers requesting a flight attendant or the pilots and flight attendants communicating with one another.

Understanding Cruising

Once the airplane reaches cruising altitude, it may feel as if it's slowing down, due to changes in engine speed. However, the plane is still moving with great velocity. These changes are normal and need to follow regulations, while providing for your safety.

The captain will make an announcement once you reach cruising altitude and you will be permitted to take off your seat belt and move around the cabin or use the lavatories. Remember to keep your seat belt fastened while in your seat just in case there is unexpected turbulence.

Depending on the length of your flight, the flight attendants will begin the in-flight service once you reach cruising altitude.

You will feel some altitude changes; this is normal. If you experience turbulence and the captain finds that it will be sticking around for a while, he or she will make an announcement informing you that the crew will be trying a different altitude. This is for your comfort and safety so don't be alarmed.

The majority of your flight will be cruising. Sip water throughout your flight so you do not get dehydrated. You may have other drinks in between, but remember that you need water. I've had many individuals try to calm their anxiety with alcohol, which is not the answer. Alcohol used as a relaxant can make you more anxious, tired and dehydrated, which can interfere with your cognitive process.

Cruise is the safest part of flying. Only about 8 percent of all accidents occur during this phase. Approximately 30 percent of all fatal accidents occur during takeoff and climb and nearly 50 percent during descent, approach and landing.[1] Because so few accidents happen during cruise, long flights are no riskier than short ones.

Understanding Touchdown or Landing

Like takeoff, touchdown (or landing) can be one of the most nerve-racking parts of air travel. This is where you may hear rattling, vibrating, roaring, grinding, clicking, drilling or squealing sounds.

The engines may sound like they are shutting down, but they aren't; they are throttled back to prepare for landing. Your ears may pop, so remember to chew gum, move your jaw and swallow hard, yawn and use the *Valsava Maneuver*: hold your nose shut and then blow gently as if you were exhaling. The back pressure can force open your Eustachian tube.

You can also ask the flight attendant to wet two paper napkins with hot water and place each at the bottom of a cup. Then place the cups over your ears on takeoff or descent. The moisture and heat helps open your Eustachian tubes and it feels somewhat comforting.

When the spoilers (speed brakes) are deployed, you may feel a vibrating sensation. This is common.

Planes may be put into a holding pattern, where the flight crew will fly the plane in circles or vectors (zigzag patterns). Today, though, most outbound planes hold on the ground so incoming aircraft can land.

The captain will announce, "We have begun our final descent into (the name of your destination)." Do not be alarmed if you feel a descent happening and no announcement was made. This is not uncommon. The descent can begin thirty to forty-five minutes prior to your arrival time. Descending or landing can vary depending on the terrain, weather, runway traffic and many other factors.

If it is a steep descent and you feel uncomfortable, you don't have to look out your window. You can do a guided imagery exercise, engage in meditation, say a prayer or close your eyes, relax and think of something pleasant.

Fear of Terrorist Attacks

Terrorist attacks have been a worry for many since 9/11. In April 2011, President Barack Obama informed the nation that a United States-led operation in Pakistan had resulted in the death of al Qaeda leader Osama bin Laden. President Obama stated, "Justice has been done."

"Though bin Laden is dead, al Qaeda is not," said CIA Director Leon Panetta. "The terrorists almost certainly will attempt to avenge him, and we must—and will—remain vigilant and resolute. But we have struck a heavy blow against the enemy."[2]

The United States has a new system which went into effect in April 2011. The Bush-era color-coded threat level system was replaced with a two-tiered system: the threat level can be either "elevated" or "imminent." With stricter security screening, a more simplified threat alert system and increased safety from terrorists, air travel (or any type of domestic or international travel) can only improve. There will always be someone or some group who may threaten, but the security systems in place and the awareness of society make it that much safer. Stay alert, be aware and follow all the instructions. If you see any suspicious behavior, be sure to report it to a flight crew member or an authority figure.

You must be patient while airport security does their work to protect you. Lines may be long, there may be delays, but isn't your safety worth it? You don't know what will happen. I won't try to paint an unrealistic picture; my clients respect and trust me for this. Have you ever crossed a street? You could have been hit by a car, but you crossed! Have you ever walked outside and got into your car during a thunderstorm? You could have been struck by lightning, but you went out to your car anyway! Be cautious, but don't live in a world of "What Ifs?" Anticipatory anxiety will only paralyze you.

Right after 9/11, I flew to St. Louis and noticed the enhanced security procedures. At the ticket counter, I was asked if anyone had access to my luggage other than myself. Several times we were informed that all carry-on and personal items must remain in our possession. One would not even think of leaving one's belongings to toss a gum wrapper into the trash. A thorough examination of my picture ID (driver's license) took place three different times: by the ticket agent, at the gate and at boarding. All told, I felt quite assured and comfortable with my observation of the security procedures. What was once taken for granted in the airline hiring process will never be again. For security personnel and crew members, background checks, educational requirements and credit history reports are all mandatory. We have transitioned into a world of caution, but a world better prepared to provide for our safety.

Many fearful flyers are concerned about bombs. The bomb detector at most airports is known as the CTX 5000 and it is certified by the FAA. It uses the same technology found in a CT-Scan. Also, dogs are trained to detect explosives.

A terrorist attack, unfortunately, can happen anytime or anywhere. But you don't stop living your life. So why would you not fly? With all the security measures in place, flying is the safest it has ever been. The government is working hard and is determined to provide for the safety of airline passengers.

Transportation Security Administration (TSA)

All passengers must pass through security checkpoints to have access to the departure gate. Give yourself ample time, because the lines can be quite long. The airlines request that you be at the airport two hours prior to your departure.

TSA has put the following notice online for your safety: "TSA and our security partners conducted extensive explosives testing since August 10, 2006 and determined that liquids, aerosols and gels, in limited quantities, are safe to bring aboard an aircraft. The one bag limit per traveler limits the total amount each traveler can bring. Consolidating the bottles into one bag and X-raying them separately from the carry-on bag enables security officers to quickly clear the items." The TSA has developed the 3-1-1 system:[3]

"3-1-1 for Carry-Ons"

3-1-1 for carry-ons: **3**.4 ounce (100ml) or less (by volume) bottles; **1** quart-sized, clear, plastic, zip-top bag; **1** bag per passenger placed in screening bin. One quart bag per person limits the total liquid volume each traveler can bring. The 3.4 ounce (100ml) container size is a security measure.

Be prepared. Each time TSA searches a carry-on it slows down the line. Practicing 3-1-1 will ensure a faster and easier checkpoint experience.

3-1-1 is for short trips. If in doubt, put your liquids in checked luggage.

Declare larger liquids. Medications, baby formula, baby food and breast milk are allowed in reasonable quantities exceeding three ounces and are not required to be in the zip-top bag. Declare these items for inspection at the checkpoint. Officers may need to open these items to conduct additional screening.

Prohibited Items for Carry-On

- Sharp objects
- Sporting goods
- Guns and firearms
- Tools
- Martial arts and self-defense items
- Explosive and flammable materials, disabling chemicals and other dangerous items

TSA Passenger Checkpoint Procedures

The passenger checkpoint includes three primary steps with which you should become familiar.

Step 1: The X-ray machine

At the passenger security checkpoint, you will place all carry-on baggage and any items you are carrying with you on the belt of the X-ray machine. You will need to lay all items flat.

NOTE: TSA will screen any carry-on baggage that will fit through the X-ray machine; however, it is up to each individual airline as to whether the baggage fits the size restrictions for your flight. Please check with the airline prior to proceeding through the security checkpoints.

Laptop computers and video cameras with cassettes must be removed from their carrying cases and placed in one of the bins provided. You will also need to remove your coat, jacket, suit jacket or blazer and place it in one of the bins. These items go through the X-ray machine.

"IN-OUT-OFF"

- Place all metal items **IN** your carry-on baggage before you reach the front of the line.
- Take your computers and video cameras with cassettes **OUT** of their carrying cases and place them in one of the bins provided.
- Take **OFF** your coat or jacket so that it can go through the X-ray machine. This includes, but is not limited to, trench coats, heavy winter coats, suit jackets, sport coats and blazers.

TSA Shoe Screening Policy: You are required to remove your shoes before you enter the walk-through metal detector. All types of footwear must be screened; if you do not follow this security procedure you will not be able to board your flight.

TIP: Since a thorough screening includes X-ray inspection of footwear, wearing shoes that are easily removable helps to speed you through the screening process.

Step 2: Walk-through metal detector

You will next walk through a metal detector (or you may request a pat-down inspection instead). Objects on your clothing or person containing metal may set off the alarm on the metal detector. You will undergo additional screening if you set off the alarm or if you are chosen for additional screening.

TIP: Pack all metal items, including the contents of your pockets, in your carry-on baggage. Mobile phones, pagers, keys and loose change are examples of items containing metal.

Step 3: Additional screening

Additional screening occurs when an individual sets off the alarm on the metal detector or if he or she is selected for the additional screening. This screening includes a hand-wand inspection in conjunction with a pat-down inspection that includes the torso.

If you must go through additional screening, the screener will direct you from the metal detector to a screening station where he or she will brief you on the next steps. At this time, you should let the screener know of any personal needs you may have due to a religious or cultural consideration, disability or other medical concern. Except in extraordinary circumstances, a screener of your gender will conduct your additional screening. You may request that your search be conducted in private.

While you will be separated from your carry-on baggage during this process, every effort will be made to help you maintain visual contact with your carry-ons.

Carry-On Baggage

If your baggage is selected for additional screening, it may be opened and examined on a table in your presence. Please do not attempt to assist the security officer during the search and do not attempt to retrieve the item before the security officer has advised you that the search is complete and your baggage is cleared.

Your baggage might also be inspected with an Explosive Trace Detection machine (ETD), which is separate from the X-ray machine.

Hand-Wand Inspection

The hand-wand inspection helps the screener to identify what may have set off the alarm on the metal detector.

During the wanding procedure, you will be asked to stand with your feet apart and the screener will pass the wand over your entire body without actually touching you with the wand. Every effort will be taken to do this as discreetly as possible.

Areas of the body that have body piercings, thick hair, hats and other items may require a pat-down inspection. You may ask to remove your body piercing in private as an alternative to the pat-down search that includes the torso. The screener may ask you to open your belt buckle as part of the process. The screener may request that you remove your shoes and your shoes may be X-rayed separately.

TIP: It is recommended (but not a requirement) that individuals with a pacemaker or any other device that is likely to alarm the metal detector bring identification verifying the condition. This may help to expedite the screening process.

Pat-Down Inspection

A pat-down inspection complements the hand-wand inspection. In order to ensure security, this inspection may include sensitive areas of the body. Security officers are rigorously trained to maintain the highest levels of professionalism. You may request that your pat-down inspection be conducted in private.

Why are some passengers patted down?

Air travelers can opt for a pat-down in security instead of a full-body scan. Those selected for additional screening may also get a pat-down. However, some feel that the pat-down violates their human rights. Consider the following example of former Miss USA Susie Castillo:

> A former Miss USA who says she was sexually violated during an airport security search has taken to the Internet with her story. Susie Castillo, 31, said on her blog she felt

> "completely helpless" and "violated" during the pat-down search by a female security guard in Dallas, Texas, earlier this month. Castillo, 31, who won the Miss USA Pageant in 2003, said she was hand-searched after she refused to go through a full body scanner at the Dallas Fort Worth International airport. "To say that I felt invaded is an understatement," she wrote. "What bothered me most was when she ran the back of her hands down my behind, felt around my breasts, and even came in contact with my vagina! I just kept thinking, what have I done to deserve this treatment as an upstanding, law-abiding American citizen? Am I a threat to US security? I was Miss USA, for Pete's sake!"[4]

According to the US Transportation Security Administration (TSA), in the United States, pat-downs are done if passengers refuse to walk through a full-body scanner, if something unusual is found on a scan or if someone sets off a metal detector. An Internet "Don't Touch My Junk" campaign against pat-downs encouraged passengers flying during the Thanksgiving holiday weekend last November to refuse security pat-downs. That month, the TSA body-searched a screaming three-year-old, a search which was partially captured by a mobile phone camera. The TSA estimates that two percent of the two million passengers screened daily in the US are given pat-downs.

Are full-body scanners safe?

Full-body X-ray scanners scan through your clothes looking for hidden weapons. In response to recent threats, these scanners can also detect explosive or dangerous equipment in body cavities. They scan your skin, eyes, breasts, head, neck and the surface of your body. Mehmet Cengiz Oz, a cardiothoracic surgeon, author and host of *The Dr. Oz Show*, which focuses on medical issues and personal health, explored the safety of these airport scanners. He found:

- When you go to the dentist, the X-ray scanner gives 1,000 units of radiation.
- CT scans give 10,000 units of radiation
- Airport scanners appear safe, giving 0.10 units of radiation.
- Those who should avoid the airport X-ray scanners are those over sixty-five years of age, cancer survivors, pregnant women and children.

Nearly 85 percent of air passengers questioned in a global Ipsos/Reuters poll in early 2011 said the measures, which were considered by some to be a violation of human rights, were warranted but a hassle, although 40 percent of travelers said they would not catch anyone determined to cause harm. Nearly a third said security procedures were too invasive.[5]

MAPPING YOUR CIRCLE OF WORRIES

This exercise will help you determine what worries you the most. Place yourself in the center circle, then the most troubling worry in the circle closest to you and work outward. Your circles will change as you work on your worries. The goal is to turn your worries into positive thoughts.

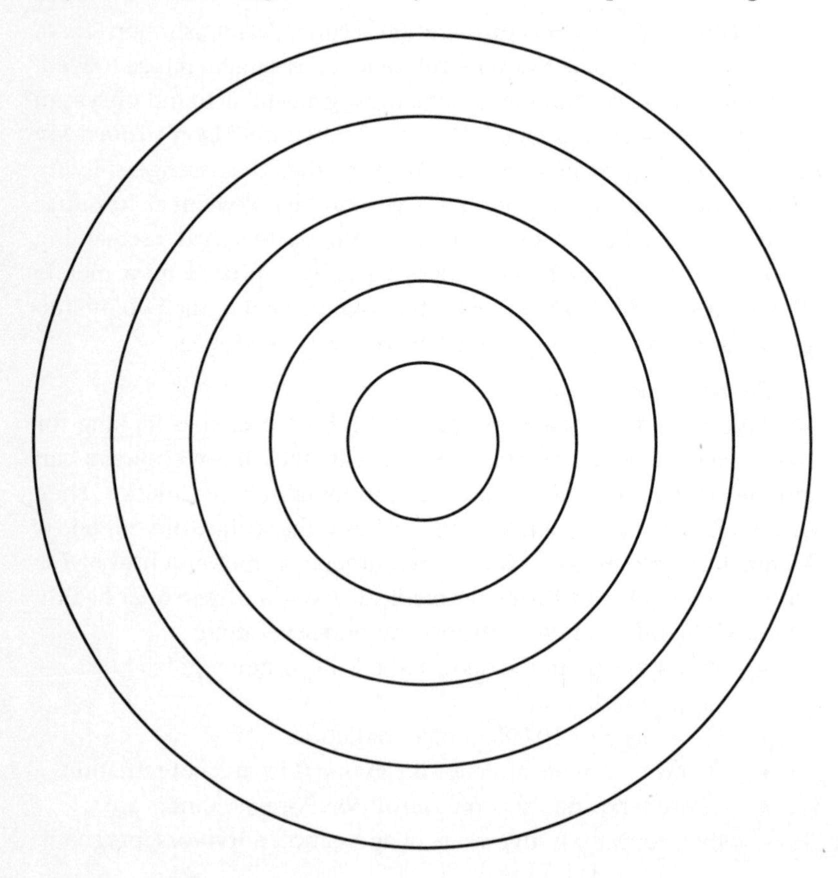

Points to Remember

We have discussed the common worries most fearful flyers have. We can't control birds, thunderstorms, tsunamis, turbulence, the plane's takeoff and landing conditions or terrorists, but the crew is well-trained to handle the plane. There are many changes currently taking place in the airline industry. There is always room for improvement; that doesn't mean that flying isn't safe at present, but it will only become better, offering you more comfort and safety for your flights. New equipment will be used to prevent anyone who is not who he or she says he or she is from flying. Even though newer safety regulations prohibit some past conveniences, remember that it's for your safety.

Key Questions

1. Do you have any of the seven common fears and have those fears started to dissipate?
2. How does turbulence affect your flight?
3. Are you prepared to go through security checkpoints and do you recognize their value?

chapter 5

Managing the Physical Toll of Flight Fear

chapter goals:

To address the symptoms of fear of flying by providing a checklist.

To provide you with tips for healthy air travel.

Through observation, experience and research, I have found many fearful flyers who worry about experiencing a possible emergency in-flight due to their medical conditions (e.g., heart problems, asthma, diabetes, ophthalmic migraine headaches, epilepsy, thyroid issues, hypertension, seizures, inner ear disorders, even pregnancy). This specific fearful flyer population may find preparation and information, psycho-education, consultations with their physicians, diet modification and a review of preventative techniques and holistic approaches helpful for flying without fear.

Physical Symptoms of Flight Fear

Your body may experience various symptoms that are produced by the fear of flying. If you don't understand them, they can be frightening, such as panic attacks.

Effects associated with fear of flying include those that influence the ***autonomic nervous system** (ANS)* and the ***sympathetic nervous system** (SNS)*. The ANS regulates certain body processes, such as the rate of breathing and blood pressure. This system works automatically (autonomously), without a person's conscious effort. The SNS activates the body's reserves under stress and stimulates the *fight-or-flight* response. Many individuals who suffer from flight fear and those with anxiety disorders experience fight-or-flight, or acute stress response, which is the root of anxiety. This is what protects animals when faced with real, immediate threats. Aviophobes perceive there is danger and their anxiety may occur from fight-or-flight or acute stress.

The systems associated with fear of flying include: Neurological and Brain Functioning, Cardiovascular System, Respiratory System, Auditory System, Ophthalmic System, Musculoskeletal System and Gastrointestinal System.

Systems and Associated Symptoms

❖ ***Neurological and Brain Functioning***
- Difficulty concentrating
- Racing, irrational thoughts
- Forgetfulness (short-term memory loss)
- Out-of-body experience; observing one's self
- Dizziness and vertigo (sensation of the environment spinning)
- Fainting
- Difficulty speaking coherently
- Difficulty making decisions; unorganized and disoriented

❖ ***Cardiovascular System***
- Tachycardia (racing pulse)
- Palpitations/irregular heartbeat (MVP)
- Hypertension (elevated blood pressure)

❖ ***Respiratory System***
- Shortness of breath
- Hyperventilation (rapid breathing)
- Tightness in throat and chest (constriction)
- Asthmatic symptoms
- Dry coughing (tickle in throat)
- Runny or dry nose

❖ ***Auditory System***
- Selective hearing due to fear
- Sounds of the airplane contribute to or increase fear

- Tinnitus (ringing in ears) or ear blockage due to flight
- Dull to severe ear pain on landing

❖ *Ophthalmic System*

- Blurred vision
- Ocular migraines
- Dry and/or irritated eyes (if you usually wear contacts, we recommend wearing your glasses)
- Itchy eyes

❖ *Musculoskeletal System*

- Muscle tightness
- Neck, shoulder and back tightness/pain
- Muscle cramps
- Toe and/or leg spasms
- Uncontrollable shakiness of legs
- TMJ discomfort (acute pain in the temporomandibular joint that connects the mandible to the skull; can be treated by your dentist and/or a neurologist)
- Headache
- Tooth pain
- Pain in the buttocks/piriformis muscle (Piriformis Disorder): a sudden involuntary contraction of the buttocks muscles. Get out of your seat and move around.

❖ *Gastrointestinal System*

- Nausea and/or vomiting
- Queasiness/butterflies
- Diarrhea
- Irritable Bowel Syndrome (IBS): Stress can worsen IBS. Nerves of the autonomic nervous system connect the colon to the brain; the nerves become more active during stressful situations causing contraction of the intestines and colicky pain.
- Jet Bloat (bloating gas pain). The higher the altitude, the more the gas in our bodies expands. Chewing gum helps reduce the pressure in your ears but can cause you to swallow excess air, as can drinking caffeinated sodas. Like a bag of chips that inflates like a pillow, most of us have 400 milliliters of gas, about the volume of a small honeydew melon.

  - Hernia aggravation (travel lightly, avoid lifting heavy luggage)
- ***Additional Symptoms***
  - Perspiring palms
  - Tingling or numbing of hands, lips and/or other body parts
  - Face flushing or chills
  - Cold hands and/or feet
  - Trapped gases: trapped gas can occur during ascent and descent, when free gas expands or contracts in certain body cavities. Your inability to pass this gas may cause ear blockage, sinus blockage, toothache and/or gastrointestinal pain.

Colds and Flying

You *can* travel by airplane if you have a cold. The flight crew has to come to work if they get colds. You just need to prepare. If you are suffering from congestion, a decongestant is advisable or you may want to have a physician assess your condition and then follow his or her recommendations; you may need a prescription to take care of the problem before you fly.

Takeoff and descent could be a problem with congestion from cold or sinus issues. Taking a decongestant before flying, chewing gum or sucking on a piece of candy to increase swallowing can relieve pressure in the Eustachian tubes of your ears. Be careful to not suck in excessive air when you are chewing gum, which may result in jet bloat.

Note: You can choose an over-the-counter (OTC) decongestant that does not cause drowsiness. In any case, a side effect of many of these medications is dryness of your mouth and eyes, so make sure that you hydrate (drink plenty of water).

Limit your use of decongestant nasal inhalants while in-flight. However, a saline nasal spray can be helpful.

Tips for Healthy Air Travel

Ear Pain: The middle ear is connected to the throat by the Eustachian tube, which equalizes pressure. If the ear becomes blocked, you can experience pain known as *barotitis* or "middle ear block." When the airplane ascends, ambient air pressure drops, and when the airplane descends the pressure increases; ear pain may be experienced on either phase of your flight. Try to clear your ears by using these steps:

1. Move your jaw and swallow several times (you can chew gum).
2. *Valsava Maneuver*: Hold your nose shut; blow gently like you are exhaling through your nose to force open the Eustachian tubes.
3. Use a saline spray or a decongestant nose spray (not to be used too often; it may cause swelling of nasal membranes).
4. Use an oral decongestant one hour prior to departure or one hour prior to landing.
5. Avoid medications which combine pseudoephedrine with an antihistamine, especially if you have a meeting or are driving after arrival; they may cause drowsiness which could last for several hours. Most antihistamines cause drowsiness.

Sinus Pain: Known as "Barotrauma of Sinuses" in severe cases. It feels like a headache on one side of the head. Pain usually is around or above the eyes. This pain is due to atmospheric pressure changes and involves congested sinus cavities. During descent, when the pressure of the air trapped in the sinuses cannot equalize with the pressure of air in the cabin, sinus pain may be experienced. Treatment to open your sinuses: Before descent, one hour prior to arrival, take a decongestant. Can cause drowsiness!

Musculoskeletal and Joint Pain: Due to the pressurized cabin and high altitudes, some individuals may experience pain. Swelling/edema can occur in feet, ankles and hands which may cause pressure resulting in pain. While in the aircraft, it helps to stretch your legs often and get up to walk when the seat belt sign is not illuminated.

Decompression Sickness (DCS): If you are a scuba diver, this is important! *DCS* is seen in scuba divers who have made recent dives. At high altitudes, nitrogen dissolved in body tissues from the dive can begin to emerge as bubbles from tissues. This condition requires immediate medical treatment. Administering oxygen onboard could help, although hyperbaric treatment, once on land, may be required to recompress the nitrogen bubbles. Wait at least twenty-four hours following a dive prior to taking a flight to prevent DCS.

Dehydration: Drink plenty of water, approximately 8 oz./250 ml each hour. If you suffer from kidney failure, consult with your physician to determine the amount of medication. Avoid carbonated beverages, caffeine and alcohol. Dehydration can occur if you don't keep hydrated due to the airplane cabin's dry air, causing symptoms of fatigue, dizziness, headache and sometimes nausea.

Altitude Sickness: Hypoxia is an oxygen deficiency in the blood, cells and tissues that causes an impairment of function. In some cases, hypoxia can occur due to the high altitude at which the aircraft travels. The physical sensations caused by hypoxia can create panic; anxiety sensitivity (AS) is thought to drive the panic cycle.

The aircraft is pressurized, but above 8,000 feet some individuals can experience such symptoms as irritability, fatigue, headache, muscle weakness, nausea, slower or faster breathing and slightly blurred vision. Smokers can feel the effects more so than nonsmokers, because the carbon monoxide in tobacco smoke weakens the body's ability to carry oxygen through the blood. Stay calm, relax and breathe.

Hypoglycemia (low blood sugar): If you missed eating because of rushing to catch your plane or were nervous and had an upset stomach, you could experience symptoms such as irritability, muscle tension, blurred vision, headache, lightheadedness, fainting and anxiety. Make sure you eat something light and leave time to grab a snack!

Thrombosis: "Traveler's Thrombosis" can be due to lack of mobility over a long period of time. Move around, no matter how you travel, by bus, train, boat or car, or if you have a desk job. **Deep vein** or **venous thrombosis** (DVT) is when a small blood clot (thrombus) or clots (thrombi) develop(s) in the deep veins, mainly in the leg. The condition alone is not dangerous, but the complication of pulmonary embolism (venous thromboembolism or VTE), can be life threatening. While in the aircraft, it helps to stretch your legs often and get up to walk when the seat belt sign is not illuminated.

Mitral Valve Prolapse (MVP): A heart problem where the valve that separates the upper and lower chambers of the left side of the heart does not close properly. It may cause anxiety, chest pain or palpitations in-flight. Stay calm.

Asthma: A common inflammatory disease of the airways, causing bronchospasm. Symptoms include wheezing, coughing, chest tightness and shortness of breath. Anxiety can bring on symptoms. If you use an inhaler for asthma, be sure to take it with you.

Allergies and Allergic Reactions: You may suffer from allergies to foods, perfumes, cleaning solutions, plastics, medications, etc. This can cause distress, embarrassment and anxiety. Consult your physician. It may be helpful to carry with you an antihistamine or whatever your doctor prescribes or recommends.

Stay relaxed if you develop any of these maladies. Being prepared will help lower your risk.

List Your Medical Concerns

Write down any medical concerns here and determine if they may cause an issue during future flights. If so, develop a plan to put in place.

____

____

____

____

____

____

____

____

____

Medical Emergencies In-Flight

A survey of European airlines identified ten thousand in-flight medical emergencies during a five-year period.[1] The study noted that each airline had its own reporting system and protocol. While emergency medical kits are required to contain certain medications and equipment, the actual kits vary from airline to airline. The FAA mandates that flight attendants receive training "to include performance drills, in the proper use of AEDs (automated external defibrillators) and in CPR (cardiopulmonary resuscitation) at least once every 24 months." Nevertheless, the FAA "does not require a standard curriculum or standard testing." Several airlines have contracts with commercial on-ground support companies, which can offer radioed, real-time medical advice.[2]

Many years ago there was a pregnant woman who went into labor in-flight. As the flight attendants had just completed their in-flight meal service, a call came over the intercom: "Is there a physician onboard?" One internist, traveling to a conference, came through the cabin and a flight attendant helped move the pregnant woman to the first class section. The physician assessed her condition as the flight attendant provided the physician with the emergency medical kit. The flight attendants were moving around the cabin, making sure the other passengers were not alarmed. After some time, the captain's voice came over the PA: "This is your captain, nothing to be alarmed about; it's a boy! We will be making an emergency landing for mom and her new son to be met by the ground medical crew. It shouldn't take us long; you should all be able to make your connections and the crew will provide you with assistance for meeting your needs. Sit back and relax." After the landing, the ground medical crew assisted the woman and her new baby. The cabin crew recorded the name and contact information of the physician as the passengers cheered for mom, baby, doctor and crew. I was the flight attendant (and nurse) who assisted with the birth of that sweet "air-born" baby.

Note: If needed, pilots also will divert a flight to the closest airport with a hospital or other medical facility nearby.

Points to Remember

Your body can experience various symptoms that are produced by fear of flying. If you don't understand them, they can be frightening.

Associated effects of fear of flying include those produced by the ***autonomic nervous system*** *(ANS)* and the ***sympathetic nervous system*** *(SNS)*. Being knowledgeable in all aspects of flying can help you become a qualified passenger, lowering your stress and making you more comfortable.

Takeoff and descent could be a problem with congestion from cold or sinus issues. Taking a decongestant before flying, chewing gum or sucking on a piece of candy to increase swallowing will relieve pressure in the Eustachian tubes of your ears. If any problem persists after you have tried all these procedures, see a physician. It is unlikely that you will experience a problem, but by having these helpful tips you will be prepared for your flight.

If there is an emergency onboard the plane, the crew is trained in first aid and there is emergency equipment on each aircraft. While emergency medical kits are required to contain certain medications and equipment, the actual kits vary from airline to airline.

Key Questions

1. What can you do for ear pain while on the airplane?
2. Have you experienced any of the physical symptoms of flight fear and how do you plan to help alleviate them?
3. What medical concerns do you have that may interfere with air travel?

PART II

Air Travel Safety Facts

chapter 6

Air Travel Statistics

chapter goals:

To introduce statistics regarding air travel.

To inform you on airline safety and jet lag.

To provide knowledge for a successful flight without fear.

It helps to look at hard numbers when dealing with a fear of flying. Use the statistics in this chapter to ease your concerns about air travel.

Safety Statistics

- One in six Americans is uncomfortable with air travel.
- The National Institute of Mental Health (NIMH) places fear of flying (acrophobia) second only to fear of public speaking.
- More than twenty-five million Americans fear flying.
- Fearful flyers tend to be perfectionists, intelligent and successful.
- The probability of being killed in an airplane crash is one in eleven million while flying domestically. If you're flying internationally, your chances of being killed in a crash are one in forty-four million.
- Flying is considered one hundred times safer than driving a car.
- A four-engine jet can land safely on just one engine.

- Planes are designed to cast off lightning.
- It is very rare that a plane has a tire blow out, because the tires are dozens of layers thick.

What Are the Safest Commercial Aircraft?

Statistics state that the safest types of airplanes are: **Airbus A330, Airbus A340, Boeing 777, Boeing 717, and Boeing 737 (600-900 series)**. An airplane is safe, because it's structurally sound and well-maintained. There is also the added safety of an experienced, well-trained crew that can handle the aircraft in any given situation.

The Consumer Warning Network (CWN) reports that in 2008, United States passengers traveled 798 billion miles by air and three trillion miles by automobile. The calculation suggests the odds of a fatal auto accident driving between Boston and Washington, D.C., are eight and a half times greater than the odds of a fatal airplane accident. Their statistical findings rank the top eight airlines in the United States (those having greater than two million flights per year):[1]

1. Southwest Airlines, 0.00 fatalities per million miles traveled (no history of fatalities)
2. Delta Airlines, 0.17
3. Northwest Airlines, 0.21
4. Continental Airlines, 0.24
5. US Airways, 0.20
6. United Airlines, 0.31
7. Alaska Airlines, 0.33
8. American Airlines, 0.40

This is an average of 0.24 fatalities per million miles traveled.

The top five foreign airlines are:

1. British Airways, 0.17
2. SAS, 0.19
3. Lufthansa, 0.22
4. All Nippon Airlines, 0.22
5. Air France, 0.72

Airplanes ranked with the best safety records (those flown greater than ten million flights per year) are:

1. Airbus A320, 0.13
2. ATR 42/72, 0.33
3. Boeing 737, 0.36
4. Boeing 767, 0.40
5. Boeing 747, 0.76

In the June 2011 issue of *Consumer Reports* magazine, 15,000 passengers cast their vote to determine the best and worst airlines. Out of the ten airlines in the survey, Southwest Airlines and JetBlue were the most popular (the votes were cast prior to the Southwest Airline accident on April 2, 2011). The least popular airlines in the report were United and US Airways (poor cabin service, baggage loss and poor entertainment service). Results found that 40 percent of people fly less due to fee increases and flight delays were a problem.

Preventing Jet Lag

Jet lag can negatively affect your air travel experience. The environmental differences related to traveling such as changes in time, alteration of magnetic fields, climate, culture, diet and a different sleeping arrangement all contribute to jet lag. It helps to set your watch to your local destination time once your plane takes off. Here are a few other tips to help you prevent jet lag:

- Exercise while in your seat; this also helps prevent blood clots and muscle pain.
- Follow a healthful diet.
- When permitted, get out of your seat and take a walk to the lavatory.
- Drink plenty of water; stay hydrated.
- If you arrive during daytime hours, stay up, get some food, take a walk or exercise and try to acclimate to the local time zone.
- Watch your caffeine, alcohol, sugar, salt and heavy fatty foods intake. You want to be able to fall asleep.

- Don't wait until your flight; adjust your diet and sleep cycle one or two weeks prior to your flight.
- Before going to bed, turn off your cell phone and pager. Inform the front desk at the hotel to call you on the house phone if there is an emergency.

Your body is programmable. Your internal cycles are like an alarm clock or computer. Jet lag will affect you physically, psychologically and emotionally. Physically, you may have some edema (swelling due to water retention); mentally, you may experience disorientation and edginess; emotionally, you may experience anxiety or stress. Follow these tips to reduce jet lag.

Jet Lag Symptoms

- Edema or swelling in your feet and/or other extremities
- Illness
- Constipation or diarrhea
- Nausea
- Clammy sweat
- Sore throat
- Dry cough
- Memory loss or confusion
- Loss of libido
- Low blood sugar
- Dizziness and/or lightheadedness
- Irregular heartbeat
- Dry skin
- Dry eyes
- Insomnia
- Irritability and impatience
- Lack of coordination
- Headache
- Fatigue

- Earache
- Hemorrhoids
- Impaired or blurred vision
- Insecurity
- Loss of balance
- Reaction to medication
- Thirst

If these conditions persist or if they appear extreme, seek medical attention as several serious medical conditions can present with some of the same symptoms. Be cautious.

Points to Remember

Air travel is statistically safe. Planes are expertly engineered and maintained. An experienced, well-trained crew who can handle the aircraft in any given situation should be reassuring. To crown one aircraft or airline as the "safest in the world" is impossible.

Our bodies need to adjust to air travel. Some quick tips to prevent jet lag: **do not nap** after you arrive; take a walk or play a game with the children or your spouse, etc. Get ready early; **condition yourself** at least one or two weeks prior to your flight. Before bed, **turn off your phone and pager.** Exercise should not be done too close to bedtime, but **exercise regularly.** For a more relaxed and stress-free flight, get **sufficient and restful sleep.** Follow a **healthful diet**; avoid caffeine, fatty foods, alcohol and excessive amounts of sugar and salt, especially the day or night prior to your flight.

Key Questions

1. What statistics did you find particularly comforting?
2. Where can you go to find more statistics regarding airline safety?
3. What causes jet lag?

chapter 7

Airline Personnel and Aviation Safety

chapter goals:

To explore the airline crew's qualifications and responsibilities to provide for your safe flight.

To help you develop trust in the airline's personnel so you will not be fearful of giving control over to them for a safe, successful flight.

Many fearful flyers are embarrassed not only about their fear to fly, but also about asking "stupid" questions. As I've always told my students, patients and clients, "The only stupid question is the one not asked!" To answer your questions and put your mind at ease, you must understand the airline industry. So let's get started and begin with the individuals in control of the plane.

Pilots

Most pilots start in their late twenties and early thirties. Pilots usually have a college education, some holding advanced degrees. They must be in excellent health with exceptionally stable personalities. Pilots must have accrued more than fifteen hundred hours of flight time, five hundred hours of cross-country flight time, one hundred hours of night flight time and seventy-five hours of instrument operations time.[1] Pilots, both male and female, are trained at civilian flight schools (e.g., Florida Institute of Technology) or in the military. The majority of commercial airline pilots begin their flying careers in the military (e.g., the Air Force Academy). Some receive training through ROTC during their undergraduate education. After meeting the requirements, fulfilling their military obligation and accumulating the required flight time, they acquire an air transport pilot license (ATP) and are able to apply for a major airline pilot position.

Those pilots who train under a civilian program can take inexpensive flying lessons which are offered by several universities. Taking the civilian route will require pilots to attain several licenses prior to receiving an ATP license. Both training routes produce good pilots and they both compete for major airline jobs. Many of these pilots gather experience and miles while working as flight instructors or flying corporate jets, commuter planes or cargo planes. Several pilots start out working for smaller commuter airlines where they obtain valuable experience flying into busy airports in all types of terrain and weather conditions. New pilots, once qualified by a major airline carrier, usually start as first officers or flight engineers.

Initial training for pilots includes one week of company instruction, three to six weeks of ground school and simulation training and twenty-five hours of initial operation experience, including a check-ride with an FAA aviation safety inspector. Once they are trained and "on the line," pilots are required to attend recurrent training and simulator checks periodically throughout their employment with the airline. Recurrent training is required twice a year. There are no inexperienced pilots in the cockpits of commercial airplanes in the United States.

Airline pilots must pass a physical exam, a drug test and psychological testing. Airlines run an extensive background check on each applicant to verify his or her credentials. After a review of the applicant's family health history, if heart disease or any other debilitating illness is found, the applicant most likely will not be hired. Also, after a complete and thorough physical, the applicant must be found to be in excellent health. Once employed by the airline, captains are required to complete physicals twice per year and first officers once per year. When captains reach the age of forty, their physicals must include an electrocardiogram (EKG) that is administered by an FAA-assigned physician. The extensive battery of psychological tests is designed to assess pilots' aptitude and the stability of their personalities. Airline pilots must be psychologically fit to handle stressful situations and the demands of the position. Each applicant will undergo a laborious interview by a panel of pilots as they are evaluated for hire.

Major airlines will hire new pilots as first officers, where they will sit in the right seat in the cockpit and alternate flying the plane with the captain. The captain is responsible for the airplane, the crew and the cargo. However, Crew Resource Management training, utilized by all domestic airlines, teaches captains how to involve their flight crews in the decision-making process. If one crew member is aware of something, he or she can voice his or her input. For first officers to advance to captain, seniority and retirement of existing captains will allow them the opportunity.

Most airlines provide uniforms and allowances for their cleaning. An attractive benefit is that pilots and their immediate families are entitled to reduced fare or free transportation on their airline or other carriers. Many airline pilots belong to unions. Most are members of the Airline Pilots Association International. Those employed by American Airlines are members of the Allied Pilots Association. Some flight engineers are members of the Flight Engineers International Association.

If a crew member or first officer is upgrading to a different airplane or moving into a new position (e.g., captain) he or she must receive upgrade training. Because cockpits differ depending on the airplane, pilots are restricted to flying one type of aircraft to ensure the safety of their passengers and crew (except for the Boeing 757 and 767, whose cockpits are identical).

There are many restrictions when the crew members, mainly the captain, first officer and flight engineer sign in for a flight.[2] The captains put their FAA licenses on the line by agreeing to the following:

- They are not using medication of any kind.

  Special FAA aero-medical approval is required to take medications of any sort, including over-the-counter (OTC) cough suppressant or allergy medications. Medications for problems such as hypertension (high blood pressure) and major heart medications would have prevented clearance for employment or continuation of employment due to safety concerns.

- They have not consumed any alcohol.

  Previously, it was against the law to drink alcohol less than eight hours prior to departure. Today, regardless of the time elapsed, your body should be alcohol-free to safely operate an airplane. Apart from the safety issues and criminal penalties, the airline will fire the offender and terminate the other flight crew members for not preventing the abuser from flying. Since 1989, crew members have been subject to random drug testing.

- They certify that they have not gone scuba diving or donated blood within the past twenty-four hours.
- The captain and first officer, within six hours of takeoff, cannot eat the same meal from the same kitchen (galley) due to concerns about food poisoning.
- When signing in, pilots also certify they are not violating any FAA-mandated fatigue restrictions.

  The Federal Aviation Regulations stipulate for safety that a pilot may not fly more than thirty hours in seven consecutive days, more than one hundred hours in a calendar month and more than one thousand hours in a calendar year. These are flight time hours, not "duty" hours, like when a pilot must stay overnight for a round trip.[3]

- When signing in, crew members must have their FAA licenses, medical certificates and FAA radio-telephone licenses.

Let's look more in-depth at issues concerning drug use and alcohol since this is a vital worry for many fearful flyers. Pilots who are caught using illegal drugs are dismissed immediately. Pilots are subject to random drug testing and testing "for cause" (e.g., pilots who are in accidents are necessarily tested).

How do random drug tests work?

- A computer randomly picks airline employees for testing.
- An airline official will meet the incoming plane and inform the pilot that he or she is to be tested and gives the details of where and when the test will take place.

- The pilot will show up at the designated facility and provide a urine specimen.
- The urine specimen is divided into two samples, so that in the event that the first test comes back positive, a second test can be run.
- Urine samples are then sent to a laboratory to be tested.
- The pilot is notified of the results. Again, if pilots test positive for drugs, they are immediately dismissed from their positions. If the samples tested positive, the pilot has the right to appeal. They may have legitimate reasons, such as drinking herbal teas or eating anything that contains poppy seeds, which can result in a false positive. Also, certain medications such as morphine-based anesthetics, which may be used in dental procedures, can test positive.

Crew Problems with Alcohol Abuse

Until January 1995, airlines depended on self-monitoring and crew monitoring. Pilots were to seek help if they were abusing alcohol and determined that it interfered with functioning on the job. Airlines are resorting to random testing of their flight crews to prevent the use of alcohol and drugs. Crew members are responsible for monitoring one another. If a crew member is aware of another crew member drinking while on the job or under the influence of alcohol and does not report it, he or she, too, may be let go along with the offending crew member. Also, flight attendants have a duty to report. Some airlines and the FAA have a hotline that can be used by any crew member or the public to report pilots who partake in any mind-altering substance, such as alcohol or drugs.

In 2002, two America West pilots were arrested and charged with operating an aircraft while intoxicated. Both their licenses were immediately revoked. They were tried and convicted in 2005. The captain was sentenced to five years in prison and the first officer received a sentence of two years and six months. In February 2003, a pilot failed a breath test just before he was due to fly across Europe and was subsequently dismissed. The FAA and the airlines have continued to clamp down on substance abuse.

FAA rules state that flight and cabin crew should not commence duty for at least eight hours after taking lesser quantities of alcohol and equivalently longer if greater amounts have been consumed. Several airlines follow stricter policies (e.g., some airlines do not allow their pilots to drink twenty-four hours before a flight and when on layovers; pilots on multiple-day trips will stay overnight in hotels to rest prior to their next flights out). In my research, I have found no airline accidents involving drugs or alcohol. Many airlines have reported wholly negative results on drug testing for their pilots (e.g., American Airlines, with almost eight thousand pilots, has never had a positive drug test). Pilots report that alcohol abuse is not a problem in the cockpit.

Captains have a lot of responsibility so they are continually screened, monitored and retrained. They and the rest of the crew are well-trained to provide for your safety and are intent on doing what they can to make your flight as comfortable as possible.

The most crucial segments of a flight are takeoffs and landings, so the captain and the first officer alternate flying different segments, or *legs,* of a flight in order to decrease the stress. You may be on a two-hour trip or even a four-hour trip, but the flight crew may be flying several legs a day, which may be up to four takeoffs and landings if not more. So the pilots' union usually restricts their number of hours flown to as low as seventy-five hours per month (remember, the FAA restricts pilots to one hundred hours of flying time per month.) The good part of the job is that the crew has shorter work weeks than many other professions. One concern is that we see pilots flying for commuter airlines making several legs per day, which includes several takeoffs and landings. The FAA has considered changing the commuter airlines guidelines for their pilots' work conditions.

Many wonder how pilots can fly long transoceanic and transcontinental flights while handling time zone changes, fatigue and mental stress. Airlines, the FAA and unions have worked together to lower the stress and fatigue of these flights. There is an extra pilot on these long flights, like those from America to Europe, along with an extra crew member for even longer flights like those to Australia or Tokyo. In some aircraft, bunks are provided for the crew members to get rest. Also, there are extra seats in the passenger cabin, reserved for the crew members to rest. The FAA realizes that it can be difficult to stay awake on these longer flights, so they are looking to allow the crew to take power naps during the flight, while one crew member will stay awake and fly the plane. The plane, for most of the longer flights, is on autopilot, so the crew's main duty is to monitor the autopilot while providing for the safety of their passengers. Many of my clients ask, "What if they fall asleep? Then what will happen to the plane?" My research found that there have not been any U.S. aircraft in an accident due to the crew falling asleep. Even if a crew member were to fall asleep, there are warning chimes to alert the crew and backup systems to secure the airplane's safe flight. We will discuss this further in chapter 8.

The crew is supervised with random line checks both by company supervisors and the FAA. The person conducting the line check unexpectedly shows up, presents his or her badge or credentials and informs the crew that he or she will be flying with them for the day. Each individual crew member's work is monitored as is the teamwork of the crew. At the end of the flight, feedback is provided by the person conducting the line check. If he or she observes a problem, he or she has the authority to have the crew member report back to the airline's training center for further training. An airline captain must have at least one line check per year or the captain's license will be suspended until the line check is conducted.

Pilots' Duties

Pilots are required to arrive at the aircraft one hour prior to departure. The junior member—the first officer or co-pilot, if it's a two-man crew, or the flight engineer if there are three—is responsible for the flight crew's walk-around, which usually occurs after the mechanics have inspected the plane.

One of the important duties of the captain and co-captain (first officer) is the double-checking of dispatch. They will pull up the weather information and scan the forecasts, winds and surface weather. Next, they will survey the dispatcher's preliminary flight plan while checking the weather reports, fuel allowance, the amount of trip fuel and the amount of hold fuel. Then the pilot will compare the information with previous history. If there appears to be any discrepancy, the pilot can request that changes be made without being questioned.

The flight crew must sign in at least one hour prior to scheduled departure time for domestic flights and one and a half hours prior to international flights. In the event that a crew member does not show up, the flight will be postponed if another qualified replacement can't take his or her place. Usually, there are crew members on call who can quickly replace the missing individual. It is an FAA rule, along with company policy, that each aircraft fly with a specific number of members in its flight crew. This is a very serious matter and strictly enforced.

The airline's Operations Department will send a flight plan, with details of the altitude and time at which the aircraft will pass over different points along the route as well as the estimated time of arrival at the destination to all the Air Traffic Control centers responsible for regulating the flow of traffic along the route the flight will be taking. Also, the Operations Department will give the time the flight must depart, so that it can be worked into the other air traffic.

The captain is responsible for his or her plane. If there is a problem in the cabin, the captain must be notified immediately. He or she will make the final decision on how the problem will be resolved (e.g., illness, threat, irate passenger, electrical problem, etc.). The flight attendants are trained to handle many situations, but the captain must still be notified.

You may see pilots carrying a large, heavy briefcase; this is known as the *Flight Kit.* In the briefcase is the pilot's operating manual, charts, diagrams, normal and abnormal procedures, descriptions of the individual aircraft systems, the operating pilot's reference book and the navigational charts. These items are frequently revised and kept up-to-date with new and necessary information. On a line check, the person conducting the inspection will usually ask to see the flight kit to make sure everything is up-to-date. Recently, United, Continental and Alaska Airlines announced plans to replace the thousands of pages in their pilots' flight kits, weighing up to forty pounds, with tablet computers which weigh less than two pounds.

Flight Attendants

The airline industry is a highly competitive business and if an applicant for a flight attendant position is not well-prepared, he or she will not make it beyond the first interview. One is fortunate if his or her application is selected out of the thousands of applications airlines receive for flight attendant positions.

Most people do not realize that the primary job of the flight attendant is to provide safety for the passengers. This profession attracts more applicants than there are job openings, so only the most qualified candidates are hired. More flight attendants will be needed as airlines increase their volume to meet rising demand, as the size and quantity of airplanes in operation increases.

Flight Attendant Qualifications

All flight attendants must be over eighteen and possess a high school diploma or equivalent. Many applicants have college degrees as well as experience in customer service and first aid. Many airlines feel that a college education and real-world experience indicate that an applicant can handle the challenges of being a flight attendant.

To be hired by a U.S. airline, one must be fluent in English. For international airlines, it helps to be fluent in a second language. Flight attendants must be United States citizens to work in the U.S.

Flight attendant applicants are vigorously screened. All applicants must clear a background check, fingerprinting, drug test and criminal record check. If hired, flight attendants are routinely re-checked. Flight attendants must be in excellent health and are required to achieve certain physical requirements—they must be able to lift passengers and equipment up to 150 pounds, they must be tall enough to reach the overhead compartments and small enough to fit on the plane, etc.

In addition to the rigorous safety standards flight attendants must meet, they are required to maintain a clean, professional appearance.

How Are Flight Attendants Trained?

Flight attendant training not only concerns service and comfort but also focuses mainly on safety. Flight attendants are trained in areas such as first aid, self-defense and emergency situations as well as customer service, culinary arts and etiquette. Training is not an easy task. A flight attendant's training is like boot camp, culinary arts program and graduate school condensed into a four to seven-week period. Flight attendants must demonstrate that they can evacuate a plane in ninety seconds with half or more of the exits blocked. They also return for training that is focused on safety at least once per year. Flight attendants are trained to work well under pressure and remain calm, cool and focused.

Flight attendants are trained by professionals in the field. The classes usually take place in the airline's flight training center and have thirty to one hundred trainees. After the training period, the applicants are then considered employees of the airline, attend a graduation ceremony and receive their wings.

A flight attendant trainee will learn emergency procedures such as evacuating airplanes, operating emergency systems and equipment, administering first aid and implementing water survival tactics. They are taught how to deal with disruptive passengers as well as hijacking and terrorist attacks. Trainees learn flight regulations and duties as well as company operations and policies and are given instruction on personal grooming. Trainees for international flights are given additional instruction in passport and customs regulations.

Flight Attendant Training Program

Flight attendants must know this information:

- City codes
- Time computations (adding/subtracting hours and minutes)
- Twenty-four-hour clock
- Airline terminology
- Company policy and procedures
- Aircraft familiarization
- First aid/CPR
- Evacuation drills/commands
- Security/bomb threats
- Uniform regulations
- Specific aircraft training
- Non-specific aircraft training
- Martial arts/self-defense
- Cabin service

- Food and beverage preparation
- Communication skills

In addition to this training, flight attendants must receive twelve to fourteen hours of training each year in emergency procedures and passenger relations.

Crew members adapt and learn to work with new crew members regularly. Flight crews change monthly. Flight crews bid on lines (trips) each month. The more seniority the better the line one can hold. A crew member can pick up a flight if the original crew member is ill, training or on vacation.

The FAA has ghost riders that observe the crew without their knowledge. Crew members may be asked questions and are expected to answer accurately within a certain amount of time. Flight attendants also carry in-flight manuals with instructions and training information. Company representatives also supervise the flight attendants in-flight. Any crew member who performs poorly or functions improperly can be dismissed.

The flight attendant trainee is given tests after each segment of the training. The passing grade is usually 90 percent. Some of the airlines allow retakes and some do not. It's helpful for trainees to practice computing time and to look over airline schedules to learn airport codes early.

The airlines train their flight attendants in everything they need to know. With so many changes in the airline industry and new issues that arise, flight attendants attend trainings regularly. Their flight manuals are updated on a regular basis.

Flight Attendants' Duties

The flight attendants are responsible for ensuring customer comfort and safety. Upon arrival at the airport, they are briefed by the captain and flight crew. Once aboard the aircraft, they check the first aid kits, fire extinguishers and other emergency equipment. They then assess the food and beverage supply as well as the stock of pillows, blankets, headphones and other passenger comfort items. Flight attendants greet passengers as they board the plane, assist with seat location and bag stowage and conduct safety demonstrations before the plane departs. Flight attendants are always ready to assist any passengers with special needs and they are trained to handle medical emergencies.

When the flight attendants are in the aisle demonstrating or showing the safety instruction film, they are presenting very important information for your safety regarding the safety cards kept in the seat pockets, seat belts, flotation devices, oxygen masks, exits, etc. They inspect the cabin to make sure all seat belts are fastened and the tray tables on the back of each seat are in the upright position. When the captain announces, "Flight attendants, prepare for departure," the flight attendants arm the emergency slides at each door. In the unlikely event of an emergency, the slides will deploy and passengers will be able to evacuate down the slides safely.

A Flight Attendant's Quick Reaction

Since 9/11, flight attendants have been trained in martial arts and self-defense. The alertness and quick reaction of the flight attendants on American Airlines Flight 63 in December 2001 prevented British bombing suspect Richard Reid from igniting wires to a possibly disastrous mix of explosives in his shoe. Passengers helped wrestle Reid down to the floor, allowing the plane to land safely. Today, the public is more alert, focused and educated on air safety.

Don't forget to offer a smile back to the flight attendants—they deserve it! And remember, flight attendants are there for your safety and comfort.

Air Traffic Controllers

The air traffic controller has one of the most rewarding, prestigious positions in government. There are plenty of opportunities for advancement into management and other fields in the industry. There will be a need for thousands of new air traffic controllers as many will be reaching retirement age and a new system may be implemented soon. Air traffic controllers are thought to have one of the most stressful careers.

In 1981, President Ronald Reagan fired thousands of air traffic controllers who went on strike. Supervisors and qualified military personnel were used as substitutes. Some of the public were afraid to fly due to the rumor that the substitute air traffic controllers were incompetent and that there was a danger of midair collisions. Since the strike, many of the underlying problems were resolved. In my opinion, a major improvement resulting from the strike and its aftermath was the decision to limit the number of airborne airplanes; once the airspace is filled with the maximum safe number of planes, no others are permitted in that airspace. Most air travel delays are now on the ground, instead of in holding patterns circling around the airports.

Air Traffic Controller Qualifications

Most air traffic controllers begin training by age thirty, with a mandatory retirement age of fifty-six. Controllers must have completed a four-year college degree program or possess definitively comparable experience. All applicants must speak English and be U.S. citizens to work in the United States. Controllers are subject to background checks, regular drug testing and fingerprinting. These tests continue throughout a controller's career.

Controllers also must go through rigorous physical examinations. They must meet strict vision and hearing standards. They must be in good health; cardiovascular exams and physicals are proctored regularly. They undergo neurological and psychological testing. They must also regularly meet stress and anxiety standards.

How Stress Affects Air Traffic Controllers

Air traffic controllers are generally assertive but calm under pressure and have the ability to follow and employ rules and be flexible when necessary. Most countries regulate work hours to safeguard the controllers, so that they are able to remain focused and effective. Over the years, it has been demonstrated that when controllers remain in position beyond two hours without a break, performance can deteriorate quickly, even at low flight capacity. Therefore, many national regulations require breaks at least every two hours. However, psycho-physiological research in the United States has not supported the widespread perception that air traffic control is an unusually stressful occupation.[4] Additionally, regulations govern shift length, number of night shifts done consecutively, length of time off required between shifts, etc. An average work week for a controller is an eight-hour day, five days per week. At some facilities, one can work a compressed schedule of four ten-hour days. Usually, controllers work "on position" for ninety to 120 minutes, then they get a thirty-minute break. Consequently, controllers frequently work rotating shifts, including nights, weekends and holidays. Usually, these are scheduled twenty-eight days in advance. In most countries, the controllers' shifts are regulated to allow for adequate time off.

Because of incidents in which controllers fell asleep on the job, two controllers must now be scheduled to work together during the night shift and early hours.

Air Traffic Controller Training

Air traffic controllers must be certified under International Civil Aviation Organization (ICAO) regulations. Some train in schools while others train by fieldwork. This training stage takes between six months and three years. When assigned to a new unit, an air traffic controller must undergo additional training in that specific area. Most of this training is accomplished with on-the-job training in live situations and with actual flights, under the supervision of a qualified mentor or an on-the-job training instructor who is prepared to take over immediately if necessary. This stage of training may vary in duration from months to several years. Before the trainee can control on his or her own, he or she must pass all of the mandatory training stages. In the U.S., air traffic controller trainees are selected through a competitive federal civil service system. Applicants are required to pass a written test that measures their ability to learn the controller's duties. Those controllers with experience as pilots, navigators or military members can improve their ratings by scoring high on the occupational knowledge portion of the test. Among the aptitudes that are measured on the test are abstract reasoning and three-dimensional spatial visualization. Applicants are required to endure a one week screening at the FAA's Aeronautical Center Academy in Oklahoma City, which includes aptitude tests using computer simulators.

Air Traffic Controllers' Duties

Important qualities for air traffic controllers are intelligence and a good memory, because they constantly receive information that must be immediately grasped, interpreted and remembered. Decisiveness is required, because controllers often have to make quick decisions. Air traffic controllers must be articulate, because directions for the pilots must be given clearly and quickly. Concentration ability is crucial; among the noise and distractions, they must remain focused and make appropriate decisions at all times. The main duties of controllers are:

- Separating aircraft
- Issuing safety alerts
- Controlling the flow of air traffic for efficiency and safety
- Directing the pilots to the runway
- Alerting pilots to additional air traffic in the area
- Issuing instructions for takeoff and landing
- Prepping before the flights take off; e.g., checking weather at the departing airport and destination airport to ensure the safest route of flight and to issue any weather delays, flight information prior to takeoff, etc.
- In an emergency, maintaining contact with the pilots, assisting in overcoming any flight problems, directing flight path changes during bad weather and directing the pilots in the unlikely event of an emergency landing
- Maintaining contact with the destination air traffic control towers, so they know which flights are coming into their areas along with times of arrival

Over the years, the success of the air traffic control program has been due to improving the tools and reducing demands on controllers through use of computer-enhanced radar. In the future, the controller's position will be transformed into managing these automated systems in situations where they can't resolve a problem. The air traffic controller's position requires skills that need regular practice and training.

Changes to Air Traffic Control Regulations

There were at least six incidents in 2011 involving air traffic controllers sleeping on the job. After an air traffic controller fell asleep on duty as a medical flight was trying to land at Reno-Tahoe International Airport in Nevada with an ill patient onboard, the FAA official in charge of operations of the air traffic control system resigned.

The FAA also suspended two controllers in Lubbock, Texas, in March 2011 for not handing off control of a departing flight to the Fort Worth Air Traffic Control Center during the night shift.

Because of these incidents, FAA Administrator Randy Babbitt and Paul Rinaldi, President of the National Air Traffic Controllers Association, started visiting air traffic control facilities.[5] They informed controllers that sleeping while on duty will not be tolerated and listened to feedback. They found that during the Miami incident there were twelve controllers on duty and two managers. Fatigue is believed to be the main factor in these incidents. Air traffic controllers' schedules have been a problem. The FAA and the National Air Traffic Controllers Association conducted a new fatigue study which found that one of the most tiring schedules is when a controller works a week of midnight shifts, followed by a week of early morning shifts and then a week of swing shifts, which begin in the afternoon and end at night. The controllers don't have time to adjust to the hours. Another problem schedule is working five eight-hour workdays compressed into as few days as possible, ending a day shift at 2 P.M. and starting another shift which begins about 10 P.M. This schedule is known as the "rattler" since it comes back to bite those working it. However, many controllers like it, because after the fifth shift they have three and a half days off before reporting back to work.

The fatigue study recommends that air traffic controllers be permitted sleeping breaks of two and a half hours during overnight shifts. Because of the study, the FAA ended its procedure of single staffing control towers at twenty-six airports and a radar facility where air traffic is light between midnight and 6 A.M. The FAA also will commission an independent review of its training curriculum and qualifications for air traffic controllers.[6]

Controllers would have a minimum of nine hours off between shifts, instead of the current minimum of eight hours. And controllers could no longer be placed on an unscheduled midnight shift following a day off.

The FAA has also reinstated a program that puts air traffic controllers in the cockpit so that they can have a better understanding of the pilot's responsibilities and workload. It is a way for pilots and controllers to communicate and better understand how each plays a part in making the flight smooth and safe. The program had ended after 9/11, when new security measures were implemented that caused cockpit doors to be locked and off-limits.

In the near future, the air traffic control system will transition to satellite communication, which will reduce the possibility of human error. But until then, keep in mind that even though an air traffic controller may fail to do his or her job, pilots are trained how to land planes without assistance.

Aviation Mechanics

If a plane is not in working condition, it will not be able to fly, so the mechanics' position is important not only to keep flights on schedule, but also to provide for your safety.

Selection and training for mechanics is similar to that of pilots. Most mechanics have been trained in the military or by an FAA-approved civilian school. Requirements set by the FAA are:

An aviation mechanic must be at least eighteen years old. Applicants must have eighteen to thirty months of practical experience in aviation maintenance. Applicants must pass three types of tests to be considered by an airline or airport. Aviation mechanics must speak English and be U.S. citizens to work in the United States. All aviation mechanics are subject to a background check, fingerprinting and regular drug testing and physical examinations.

Mechanics are responsible for their work. After repairs are completed, they must sign the plane's log book, documenting their employee numbers, and a supervisor makes sure the repair was done correctly, signing the log book and writing his or her employee number with his or her signature. Mechanics undergo continuous training on an annual basis and their work is also supervised by the FAA. If they do not perform their work efficiently, they and their supervisors may be fined five thousand dollars or more.

The Pre-Flight Inspection

The exterior inspection by the mechanics is very important and happens prior to every flight. This inspection checks more than one hundred separate items. Mechanics check the exterior for any signs of damage or wear. Particular attention is given to the landing gear, tires and brakes. The engines are checked for wear and any abnormal presence of oil.

Flight controls are checked and their positions are then documented. The hydraulic systems are inspected for leaks around the pumps and actuators to find drips even before they register on the gauges in the cockpit. The fuel lines are also checked for leaks. Pressurization valves are examined. Air vents are scrutinized to ensure that they are open and clear. Service and inspection panels are inspected to ensure they are closed and locked.

During winter months, the preflight inspection will include a check to see if there is any ice or frost on the wings. If the pilot notices ice or thinks there's a possibility of it forming, the airplane will be de-iced. This is very important; ice buildup on the wings reduces their lifting ability and adds weight to the plane, which makes it more difficult to take off.

The type one fluid originally used for de-icing lasts for fifteen minutes. The newer type two fluid lasts for thirty minutes or more. Also, the aircraft has its own onboard anti-ice system. The wings' anti-ice system hot air supply, obtained from the engine compressors, reduces the power that is available for takeoff if used on the ground. This onboard anti-ice system is only used when the plane is at least 400 feet in the air and climbing.

If there's a delay on the runway and more ice forms, the plane can return to the gate for another round of de-icing. This is when you must be patient! Remember, better safe than sorry.

A newer approach to de-icing is now being tried: A separate de-icing facility is located on the taxiway, near the runway; this allows the de-icing process to take place closer to takeoff, when it will be most needed.

Aviation Mechanics' Other Duties

- ➢ Keep the airplane in safe working condition
- ➢ Service the engines, engine components and airframe components
- ➢ Identify hazardous aircraft conditions and determine when aircraft should not fly

- Modify and replace parts
- Rely on experience and judgment to plan and achieve goals

It is more cost-efficient and takes less time to replace most aircraft parts than to repair them. After a faulty part is removed from the plane, it is then shipped to a maintenance hangar to be rebuilt.

Whenever something is wrong with an aircraft, the problem is legally noted in the aircraft's log book. This log book containing the plane's mechanical history is always kept on the plane. This allows the crew to anticipate problems before they happen. When a problem does occur, the aircraft is usually taken out of service and repaired.

When the flight crew detects a mechanical problem while in-flight, they radio the problem to the maintenance coordinator via central dispatch. The local mechanics will be contacted and meet the flight with the necessary tools to replace the part or resolve the problem.

The mechanic makes the first walk-around and the co-captain usually conducts the second inspection. The mechanic inspects the exterior of the aircraft while the passengers are deplaning, then moves to the cockpit, checking the pressure and quantities of oil, hydraulics, fuel and emergency oxygen. On newer aircraft, the status computers can be accessed directly. When the mechanic is satisfied with the plane's functions and condition, he or she will then sign the log book. The plane is then free to fly its next leg or route.

So when you're sitting impatiently at the gate, wondering why the plane is still parked, remember it is for your safety. This is one of the major reasons why we fortunately hear of so few airline accidents: the crew and mechanics promptly get on the problem. Be thankful when they board your plane!

Recent Additions to Flight Crew Training

Under proposed new FAA rules, pilots will have to demonstrate their skills in flight simulators, in addition to what they have been required to do in the past, learning how to recognize and recover from problems such as aeronautic stalls or flight upsets.

Airline pilots and flight attendants will have to learn how to respond to "real world" scenarios and demonstrate their skills in flight simulators and emergency drills. Flight crews, flight attendants and ground-based airline dispatchers will train as a team on how to respond to emergencies.

These changes should contribute to reducing aviation accidents significantly. The FAA states, "178 accidents from 1988 to 2009 were the result of inadequate training, incomplete operating manuals, inadequate training standards and operating procedures. The accidents resulted in 492 fatalities, 196 serious injuries and 615 minor injuries."[7]

The proposal also will require remedial training for pilots with performance deficiencies such as failing a proficiency test or check or unsatisfactory performance during flight training or a simulator course.

The FAA is working on a separate rule to reduce pilot fatigue by regulating flight time and rest periods and also a rule setting minimum pilot qualifications.

Other Aviation Safety Jobs

By 2021, the FAA predicts that one billion passengers will be flying each year, making aviation safety careers an important role in the aviation industry. Aviation safety jobs include those that work toward the prevention and investigation of flight failures stemming from human error, mechanical malfunctions and terrorism.

Aviation Safety Inspectors

Aviation safety inspectors work for the FAA or for private airlines and airports. Their duties are to investigate, administer and enforce FAA regulations, maintain regulatory standards in aircraft production, operation and maintenance and evaluate aviation mechanics, programs, equipment and facilities. Manufacturing inspectors inspect aircraft production, parts and avionics equipment and monitor manufacturing facilities.

An operations safety inspector is required to have at least one year of pilot experience with a 12,500-pound maximum certified take-off weight, no more than two pilot-error flying accidents in the last five years, a valid second-class FAA medical certification and an Airline Transport Pilot Certificate or Commercial Pilot Certificate with instrument rating.

Federal Air Marshal

Federal air marshals are armed federal law enforcement officials deployed on flights. Their duties are to proactively fight terrorism on aircraft and conduct investigative work on land to prevent terrorist attacks.

To qualify as a federal air marshal, individuals must pass a panel interview, a psychological assessment, a medical examination, a physical training assessment and a background check.

Transportation Security Officer (TSO)

Transportation security officers (TSOs) implement Transportation Security Administration screening procedures at airports. Their duties include screening baggage, passengers and cargo at various airport security checkpoints.

To qualify as a transportation security officer, individuals must be U.S. citizens, read and speak English, possess a high school diploma or GED, have one year of work experience and pass a complete background check. Other qualifications include passing an aptitude test and a full medical examination.

Ground Operations Crew

The ground operations crew tags, loads and unloads customer luggage, operates ground service equipment and coordinates the service and surface movement of arriving and departing aircraft, helps prepare aircraft cabins for departure, assists with fleet service duties including the operation of aircraft fueling and waste disposal equipment, assists customers with special needs and complies with any ad hoc requests. The crew must follow airline rules such as undergoing physical exams and drug testing.

Customer Service Ticket Agents

Customer service ticket agents are responsible for ticketing and re-booking passengers, conducting flight boarding, assisting special needs passengers, resolving customer complaints and performing other duties as delegated. They are also responsible for presenting a consistently professional and positive image of the airline.

Points to Remember

My clients feel it is important to have a thorough understanding of the airline industry's job descriptions. It reassures them about the safety each position provides for their travels. Airline professionals must be well-qualified and must undergo continual retraining. They also submit to performance evaluations and comply with strict rules. The airlines select only the best applicants for each position. As you can see, the airline industry places safety first!

Key Questions

1. Are you more confident about air travel now that you know more about airline personnel?
2. What surprised you about crew safety?
3. How does each member of the flight crew work to ensure your comfort and safety?

chapter 8

Understanding Aircraft Equipment

chapter goals:

To address the various parts of the fuselage and the entire aircraft.

To help you become informed of and better understand the plane so that this information helps to defuse your fear.

A frequent cause of flight fear is "fear of the unknown." Some fearful flyers don't know what to expect, especially the uncomfortable feeling of shock when they board the plane and it appears much smaller or much larger than they imagined. It helps to know about different types of aircraft, their parts and variations.

Some frequently-used types of commercial aircraft are the Boeing 777, Airbus A380, Boeing MD-80, Boeing 737NG and Canadair Regional Jet (CRJ700). Let's take a closer look at each:

- **Boeing 777:** flown by airlines such as British Airways and United, it is a long-range, wide-body jet that can fly more than 11,000 nautical miles without refueling (unloaded). It is 242 feet long and can cruise at altitudes above 43,000 feet. It can go from zero to sixty mph on the ground in less than six seconds. It seats 368 passengers and the cabin is divided into three class sections.
- **Airbus A380:** flown by airlines such as Qantas, Lufthansa and Singapore Airlines, it is the largest of the Airbus jetliners. It is a double-decked, wide-body jet that can fly loaded to a

range of 8,200 nautical miles. It is 238 feet long, seats 525 passengers and provides 50 percent more floor space than any other jumbo jet. It has wider seats, larger storage spaces and extra headroom compared to other Airbus models. It offers the lowest cost per seat of any jumbo jet.

- **Boeing MD-80:** flown by airlines such as American Airlines, Swissair, Alitalia and Delta, it is a narrow-body, two-engine jet aircraft. It stretches nearly 148 feet in length and seats 172 passengers. It is a midsize plane, with a wingspan of nearly 108 feet, and it can fly up to 2,700 nautical miles before refueling.
- **Boeing 737NG:** flown by airlines such as AirTran, American Airlines, Continental Airlines, Japan Airlines, KLM, Delta Airlines, Southwest Airlines and United Airlines, it is a short to medium range, narrow-body jet aircraft with a wingspan of 117 feet and a maximum speed of 544 mph. It has a two-member cockpit crew.
- **Canadair Regional Jet (CRJ):** flown by airlines such as SAS, American Eagle, Pinnacle Airlines and SkyWest USA, it is a family of regional airliners manufactured by Bombardier, patterned on the Canadair Challenger business jet design. Depending on the model, it seats between fifty and one hundred passengers.

Remember Teri, who was afraid that the plane was going to crash and didn't like the sounds she heard when she was on a flight to California for a family vacation? Her goal was to learn about the sounds of the plane. On her flight to California, Teri was really excited but once in-flight, she heard a vibrating noise that really scared her. What she heard was vibrations and some tonal fluctuations coming from the engines. The sounds also could have come from loose articles in the galley or luggage that was not properly secured. She did state that there was some turbulence; the wing tips can flex somewhat in turbulence and are designed to do so to absorb the vibrations. Teri's seat was near the engines, which made her hear the power of the plane being reduced slightly, as when it entered turbulence. Although the sounds and turbulence were scary, being shaken a little and hearing vibration and engine changes is normal for air travel. She was much more comfortable after understanding the noises and mechanics of the airplane. During turbulence, you only need to be concerned when you are not fastened in your seat belt or if your luggage is not properly secure in the overhead compartment.

All kinds of frightening images can flash in your mind when you encounter something that is unknown. Your psyche compensates for unfamiliar sights or sounds and fills in the blanks with memories that you do know or may remember from a scary movie or book.

Common Flight Noises

Airplane noises come from various causes:

- **Vibrations** and **humming** sounds from the retraction of the landing gear.
- **Rattling** during takeoff, landing and turbulence can be caused by loose articles in the galley or by items moving in overhead bins and other parts of the cabin due to engine vibrations.
- **A loud roar following touchdown** is the sound of the thrust reversers, which help slow the aircraft after it's on the runway. They reverse the flow of the air through the engines; that's why they sound so loud. Airplanes are designed to stop using brakes alone but flight crews typically deploy the thrust reversers, helping to save wear and tear on the braking system.
- **Excessive noise** like constant roaring can occur when your seat is near the engines or near the tail of the plane. The noise level is usually higher in these two areas.
- **Power reduction engine noise** after airborne might occur in order to comply with the noise abatement procedures around certain airports.
- **Air-conditioning noise** may change to supply cooling and heating needs.
- **Grinding, clicking and squealing sounds prior to landing** come from the operation of the landing flaps.
- **A thump beneath the floor following takeoff** is the landing gear being retracted into the belly of the airplane and the doors to the landing gear bay being shut.

- **A drilling sound prior to takeoff and on approach to landing** is the sound of the flaps and slats being extended on the wings. These panels increase the area and curvature of the wing when extended to facilitate low-speed flying and are controlled by a screw mechanism which causes the noise you hear.
- **A high-pitched whine prior to takeoff** is the sound of the engines winding up for takeoff. Once airborne, the pilot will throttle the engines back and while cruising, the sound of the engines becomes more of a hum than a whine.

These noises are normal and you have nothing to worry about. If there is an abnormal noise, the flight attendants will notify the captain and he or she may inform you, in the case of such an unlikely event, as to what is going on. The flight attendants would then instruct you to provide for your safety.

How Engines Work

Many fearful flyers are concerned that the powerful engines and equipment may fall off! The truth is that they are built to stay attached. Planes are routinely inspected by trained mechanics and engineers.

To better understand the aircraft's engines, let's take a look at one of the most powerful airplanes, the 767, which has two engines. Each engine is almost nine feet in diameter, weighing more than 10,000 pounds. Each is capable of generating 60,500 pounds of thrust (24,000 horsepower). Airplanes must have these very powerful engines so that they can carry not only the large aircraft but also the weight of the passengers and their luggage.

Another concern regarding engines is the fear of birds flying into them and causing the airplane to crash. It is a concern that was aggravated in January 2009, when a US Airways Airbus A320, airborne less than three minutes, had both engines become disabled and lose thrust after striking a flock of Canada geese. The flight had to be aborted. Captain Chesley Burnett "Sully" Sullenberger III brought his aircraft and all 155 people aboard to a well-executed and safe ditching in the Hudson River. There have been several incidents in the past and birds are an ongoing concern for the FAA and the airlines. Engines can handle birds around four pounds; anything larger can cause damage, but pilots are trained to handle all situations. Birds won't necessarily clog an engine, but they can break or bend the fan or compressor blades, causing power loss or failure.

Various airports, especially those along coastal areas, use border collies, scarecrows, loud horns, whistles, bells and shotguns to keep birds from interfering with aircraft safety.

You have probably heard some myths about airplane engines such as "Engines that become older are more likely to fail," "Engines that are bigger and more powerful are more likely to fail" or "More flights and a quicker turnaround time allow less time for maintenance." First, most parts are replaced rather than repaired. But those parts that are rebuilt or modified must pass inspection and meet the same standards as parts for new aircraft. Second, size makes no difference as long as the equipment is in excellent working condition. Third, the planes are well inspected, as you can recall the walk-around made by the mechanics, captains and first officers. There are check-off lists and the FAA has strict rules that must be followed prior to each flight. While you are boarding, the ground crew, captain, first officer and mechanics are busy preparing the plane for a safe flight.

How Wings and Fuel Storage Work

The wings, just like those of a bird, help the plane glide. Different aircraft have different wingspans. For instance, the Boeing 737NG has a wingspan of 117 feet while the 747-400, with a surface area greater than a basketball court and a wingspan of over 211 feet, supports exactly the same weight per square foot (100 pounds). The wings of an airplane are not only very strong but also flexible. A 767 has a maximum gross weight of 407,000 pounds. When turbulence puts stress on the airplane's frame and wings, the plane can withstand a force of two-and-a-half times its weight.

Ailerons are movable surfaces on the trailing edge of the wings used to control the angle of bank when the plane is making a turn. The **flaps** are two sets of panels located along the backside or edge of the wings. They can move outward and downward. **Slats** are a series of panels on the front side or leading edge of the wing. They move symmetrically forward and down. On most airplanes the flaps and slats are positioned in the fully up or retracted position while at the gate.

Both slats and flaps are operated hydraulically but locked (held in position) mechanically. On the underside of the wings you can see the cover for the jack screws that turn to move the flaps. When the flaps and slats are fully extended, they increase the surface area, making it possible for the plane to fly slower, which reduces the amount of runway needed for takeoff and landing. In the unlikely event of a malfunction where the flight crew cannot get the flaps and slats out hydraulically, they can turn to a backup electrical system. If for some reason that fails, there are other systems that would enable them to bypass the faulty portion of the system and extend some of the flaps and slats. In the event of an extremely rare situation where nothing works, the plane could still land; the only difference is that it would have to land at a higher speed, requiring a longer runway and using greater braking power after touchdown.

Most of the airplane's fuel is stored inside the wings. This gives the wing extra strength. To give you a few examples: A 767 holds over 24,000 gallons of fuel. The 747-400 holds 60,000 gallons; this would permit you to operate your car for eighty years! Due to fuel prices, which rose 28 percent in 2011, some airlines have decided to cut their capacity. United Continental Airlines burns $25,000 in fuel each minute. The airline may gain efficiency by other actions, such as using only one engine while taxiing.

Many fearful flyers ask, "How long can an airplane stay in the air once it runs out of fuel?" It depends on the airplane's altitude when the fuel runs out. The higher the airplane, the farther it will glide and therefore it will stay up a bit longer. For example, if the airplane is at 35,000 feet or about seven miles high, it would glide at about five miles a minute at a descent rate of about 4,000 to 5,000 feet per minute. At this gliding speed and rate of descent, it would travel between thirty-five and forty-five miles, depending on whether there was a tail or a headwind. So it would have approximately seven minutes to make it to an airport.

Sensors and position lights are located on the tips of the wings. The left wing tip has a red light, the right one a green light. On the rear of the wing tips are white lights. These lights are turned on day and night, helping flight crews determine whether other planes are flying toward them or flying away. On the wing tips there are also strobe lights flashing forty-eight times a minute, used as anti-collision beacons. When flying through clouds, their reflections into the cabin can be mistaken for lightning. Another anti-collision light, visible from the cabin, is a flashing red rotating beacon which sits on the top and bottom of the fuselage. At night, it can be a pretty sight as you look out your window. Don't mistake the red lights for fire.

Anti-icing of aircraft, especially the wings, is done by applying a protective layer of anti-ice fluid over the plane's surface. All anti-ice fluids offer only limited protection, dependent upon the frozen contaminant type and prevailing weather conditions. The plane's onboard engine and wing anti-ice system will heat up to prevent ice buildup when operating near the freezing point and when visible moisture is present.

How Plane Tires Function

The parts that receive the most wear and tear are the plane's tires. The tires do not rotate in the air, but at touchdown they accelerate abruptly from zero to 150 mph. You can see a puff of smoke when the wheels begin to spin on touchdown. Tires on a 767 are up to thirty-two ply; a car tire has two to four plies. Tires are changed roughly every 200 landings, which averages out to every month and a half. The tires have a maximum speed of 253 mph, which is well above the requirement for takeoff and landing. Each tire has its own set of brakes, with five or more sets of discs for each tire; a car has just one per tire! Each brake has its own antiskid system.

Many fearful flyers ask, "What happens if my airplane gets a flat tire?" If the landing gear doesn't work, the runway will be prepared with a foam spray so that the airplane can make a safe emergency landing. If a Boeing 777 were to experience a single flat tire, it could still land safely, because it has a total of fourteen tires. From the cockpit, a pilot can tell which of the tires is flat. On the main landing gear, each tire has a pressure of over 200 psi (pounds per square inch). When the pressure is low or if a tire is flat, a warning will come on to inform the pilot of the situation. It is usually not a major problem. The aircraft can still land safely with one flat tire. After touchdown, the mechanics will change the tire and the airplane will make its next flight. There are alarms and backup systems for just about everything on a plane to provide for your safety.

What is the APU?

The APU (Auxiliary Power Unit) is a small engine located in the tail of most aircraft. The APU provides ground electricity and air for ground air conditioning. If a plane does not have an APU, it will be hooked up to a mobile APU until it is ready to taxi. Today, most aircraft have their own built-in units.

Flight Data Recorders (FDRs)

The **flight data recorder** (FDR), also known as the black box, is designed to record the operating data from the plane's systems. There are sensors that are wired from various areas on the plane to the flight data acquisition unit, which is wired to the FDR. When a switch is turned on or off, that operation is recorded by the FDR. Even though it is called the "black box," the FDR is actually housed in a bright orange container, able to withstand forces of 200 Gs or more and temperatures of more than 2,000 degrees Fahrenheit. It is usually mounted in the tail of the plane.

The flight data recorder has a twenty-five-hour tape that records the parameters of the flight, the time, altitude, vertical acceleration, heading, airspeed, positions, etc. It contains a water-activated transmitter that sends out signals for thirty days to assist in recovery.

An Air France Airbus A330-203 crashed into the Atlantic Ocean off the coast of Brazil en route to Paris from Rio de Janeiro in June 2009 after the flight encountered bad weather. Unfortunately, all 228 passengers and the flight crew died. Investigators believe the cause of the accident was due to the possible icing of the aircraft's speed sensors that appeared to give inconsistent readings prior to loss of communications. During an underwater remote vehicle dive in April 2011, the chassis of the flight data recorder was found. Everything that was learned from that black box has been used to help prevent similar incidents from occurring.

Cockpit Voice Recorders (CVRs)

In almost every commercial aircraft there can be up to four microphones built into the cockpit, each connected to the cockpit voice recorder (CVR), to track the conversations of the flight crew. These microphones are designed to track any ambient noises in the cockpit, such as knocks, thuds or switches being thrown.

The voice recorder records all of the conversations in the cockpit, including radio transmissions with air traffic control and the airline company, requests made to the flight attendants or conversations about a problem in-flight. In some cases the FDR and CVR may be combined in a single unit. These are very valuable pieces of equipment.

The Nose of the Plane

In the past, the black, dull painted nose was mainly to control glare from the sun. A special, anti-erosion paint was used for the nose cone, or radome. Nowadays the radome is usually painted the same color as the rest of the plane.

The weather radar antenna is right behind the radome. The radome is made of plastic (fiberglass) and the thickness has to be constant or the performance of the radar will be impaired. There are bonding strips (three silver lines) that every radome has and their purpose is to conduct static electricity and lightning to the rest of the airframe so that it can be dispelled by the static wicks. The radome can detect rain showers, thunderstorms and turbulence. It typically scans up to 320 miles in front, ninety degrees left and right and fifteen degrees up and down.

Plane Windows

Window sizes, shapes, quantity and structure vary by aircraft. Some are made of acrylic plastic, while others have strong, thick glass. (For example, the window unit of a 747 is made up of three layers. The outer pane is stretched acrylic, the middle pane is modified acrylic and the inner pane is a thin sheet of acrylic, which acts as a dust cover. They are coated for scratch resistance.) Airplane windows are designed to withstand substantial pressure; the window is surrounded by a pressure seal. Due to the shape of the nose of the 747, the forward four windows have an additional twelve retainer fittings to strengthen the window against bird strikes.

Cockpit windows are heated by two systems and they are usually larger in new aircraft. The windshield is three quarters of an inch thick and has three layers of glass, which are separated by two layers of vinyl. Most other cabin windows are double paned, with rounded corners for extra structural strength. There are window shields for protection from sunlight. These shields must be slid up during takeoff and landing due to safety regulations.

Plane Doors

Door sizes, shapes, quantity and structure vary by aircraft. One of two forward doors is usually used for boarding. The doors on an aircraft usually consist of the entry and galley doors, emergency exits and over-wing exits. When in-flight, the doors cannot open due to the cabin pressure, which tightly seals the doors. In most aircraft, evacuation slides are built into the airplane's doors and prior to pushback the flight attendants will arm their doors. The slides are armed after the airport services agent closes the forward entry door and has moved the jetway away from the aircraft. Once all the doors have been secured, the flight attendants inform the captain that the "cabin is secured for pushback."

Plane Seats

Like the carpets, ceiling and other upholstered surfaces, the seats are fireproof. Older aircraft used relaxing color patterns and earth tones and some airlines preferred leather seats due to soiling and damage concerns. There are some airlines that still use calming colored patterns, though today many airlines opt for a more business-like look with soft blues and grays.

Seats are usually arranged in rows running across the airplane's fuselage. Aircraft seats vary, depending on manufacturer, model and size. When booking your flight, check the airline's website and click on the particular aircraft model to look at the seating maps and availability. Also helpful is SeatGuru.com, which shows seat maps for a wide range of airlines and aircraft, along with descriptions of the best and worst seats on the aircraft. Due to changes in the economy and the airline industry, one does not have the luxury of flying larger planes on shorter flights, nor can some pay the cost for first class or business class, which have larger seats and more space.

The widest narrow-body aircraft, such as the Airbus A320 series and Boeing 737, have six-across seating in a three-by-three layout. Other layouts also exist, including the Embraer Regional Jets, which have a one-by-two seating layout. On wide-body aircraft the center rows of seats between the aisles can have as many as five seats on planes like some Boeing 777s.

Passengers who want to have a view or something to lean against tend to book a window seat. Passengers who like aisle seats are able to leave the seat without having to squeeze over the other passengers and can stretch their legs. But if you like an aisle seat, keep your elbows and legs tucked in when the beverage cart is coming through. Middle seats are less popular with travelers, especially fearful flyers.

Where Is the Safest Place to Sit in an Airplane?

Many individuals want to know the safest place to sit in a plane cabin. Though there is not enough empirical data to support which seating area is the safest, you can consider various factors when you select your seat:

- The airplane is quieter in front of the engines.
- The airplane is more stable near its center of gravity, the mid-section.
- The seats with the most legroom are those in the first row behind the bulkhead and in the emergency rows, although these seats do not recline and you must meet special guidelines to sit in them.
- Aisle seats are easier for getting out of your seat and walking around to stretch your legs.
- Window seats are good for a view and leaning against the wall to rest your head.
- Seats in the first row behind the bulkhead have their tray tables in the armrests, which prevents the armrests from being raised.
- There is more room in the first row behind the bulkhead when traveling with an infant. (Note: There is only one infant permitted per row, because there is only one extra oxygen mask per row.)
- First Class and Business Class have larger seats and more space, if you are uncomfortable in tight spaces.

Boeing's website states, "While some people believe the safest spot is near the wings or toward the rear of the cabin, there's no conclusive evidence to support either theory. One seat is as safe as another, especially if you stay buckled up."[1]

Special Seating Guidelines

Some passengers require special seating. If needed, the flight attendants will assist you in following the guidelines.

- Passengers seated in the exit rows must meet requirements in compliance with exit row seating standards. Those who are not permitted to sit in these rows when prohibited by the airline company's policy:
  - Passengers who require a seat belt extension or pregnant women whose condition is visible;
  - Children under the age of two;
  - Unaccompanied minors;
  - Passengers who are disabled.
- Prisoners and their guards:
  - Seated in the last available row of seats.
  - Guard sits aisle side.
  - Prisoner seated in the middle seat or by the window.
  - A customer must not be seated next to a prisoner or between a prisoner and a guard.
- Assistance animals and ticketed articles:
  - Placed in areas in compliance with procedures in company policy chapter.

Seat Belts

All seats have a seat belt that must be worn for your safety. The captain will illuminate the "Fasten Seat Belts" sign above each seat when you are expected to remain seated with the seat belt fastened, e.g., during taxiing, takeoff, landing and turbulence. It is best to keep your seat belt on while in your seat in case of unexpected turbulence. Some may find airline seat belts a bit snug; there are seat belt extensions if needed. For your safety, your seat belt should be worn low and snug at all times when seated.

Reclining Seats

Most seats are equipped with a reclining mechanism for your comfort. Some seats may not recline, like those in the rear row of the cabin where a rear bulkhead blocks the recline or the seats immediately in front of the emergency exit, where a reclined seat might restrict access to the exit. The flight attendants prefer to have passengers sitting in an exit row who are able to assist in removing the door in the unlikely event of an emergency situation. That is why these passengers are labeled Able Bodied Passengers (ABP).

During takeoff and landing the flight attendants will request that you put your seat in an upright (un-reclined) position and lift and stow your tray table as well as any carry-on luggage which you may have taken down from the overhead compartment. Most aircraft provide trays for eating and reading, either in the seatback that folds down to form a small table in most economy class seats or inside the armrest which folds out in most first class, business class, bulkhead and exit row seats. Most airline seats also provide a pocket that can be found on the back of the seat in front of you, which contains an in-flight magazine and a safety pamphlet. Take out the safety pamphlet and follow along carefully as the flight attendant demonstrates the safety procedures at the beginning of each flight.

Some business class cabins offer seats that recline to a slanted, semi-flat position. Most international first class business class cabins offer seats that recline to a fully horizontal, flat position. You have your own relaxing bed!

In 2011, Delta Airlines began the installation of thirty-four horizontal flat-bed BusinessElite seats with direct aisle access in each of thirty-two Airbus A330 aircraft. Also, the airline plans to add an "Economy Comfort" section to international flights where four inches of legroom and reclining ability will be added to the seats.

Customer Service Unit (CSU)

Directly above your seat on the cabin ceiling is a small console for your use. The controls on the CSU include:

- An air-conditioning nozzle that you can tilt, swivel and adjust either to increase or reduce the output. This feature is found on most narrow-body aircraft though many airlines have opted to omit it on many newer wide-body aircraft (e.g., Boeing 777).

- A reading light (commonly very similar in appearance to the air nozzle) that you can turn on for extra light, principally when the main cabin lights are turned off. The buttons to turn the lights on and off are generally located directly on the overhead console on most narrow-body aircraft, whereas on most wide-body aircraft, the buttons are generally found together with the in-flight entertainment controls, usually located on the armrests, on seat backs or through the touch screens on some personal televisions.
- A call button that, when pressed, alerts the flight attendants to your row. The flight attendants are notified by a small light on the console and also informed by a quiet audible tone. The call button is usually located directly on the overhead console on most narrow-body aircraft or with the in-flight entertainment controls on most wide-body aircraft.

Overhead Compartments

The overhead compartments are to store your (one) carry-on bag, if it does not fit underneath the seat in front of you. The FAA and airlines had previously permitted two carry-on bags, but due to safety reasons and cost, passengers are now limited to one. Some of the newer aircraft have more than two and a half cubic feet of overhead storage area per passenger.

Don't put anything in your baggage that could be explosive or alarming, like a ticking clock or an alarm going off while in-flight. With the strict security screenings, you most likely will not have anything that could be explosive (hairspray, lighter, etc.). Try to always travel light. It makes traveling so much more enjoyable and relaxing!

You should remain in your seat until the captain has turned off the "Fasten Seat Belt" sign and the airplane has come to a complete stop. Otherwise, you and your baggage could fall and someone could be seriously hurt. Always make sure your baggage is secured and well-stowed for safety purposes. Follow the flight attendants' instructions.

Entertainment System

Most seats are equipped with power sockets for small electrical devices and ports for headphones to listen to the audio entertainment. Also, some airlines such as JetBlue have individual TV screens in the back of each seat for in-flight entertainment on longer flights.

Audio and/or video entertainment is available on most mainline aircraft. Most airlines offer headsets for you to buy or you may bring your own.

Food and Beverage Service

In today's world of flying, if your flight is not long you will have to pay for what you eat (if food is even offered). For most airlines the days of free snacks, food and drinks are long gone! I suggest you pack a little snack for yourself, especially if you are diabetic or hypoglycemic.

Most snacks, even peanuts and pretzels, will cost you. Up until 9/11, a typical major airline had approximately 2,500 flights, serving 150,000 passengers per day. This translated into 130,000 meals and snacks and 375,000 beverages every day! It took 105,000 pounds of ice daily to chill this many beverages.

One major carrier disclosed that a fully-provisioned Boeing 747 held 491 cups, 972 plates, 847 glasses, 176 bottles of wine and 25 gallons of liquor.

Southwest Airlines was one of the first carriers that stopped serving food onboard. With the economic problems, the luxury of "meals and drinks in the sky" had to be revised or eliminated. I remember when we cooked on flights, offering meals like Beef Burgundy or Chicken Cordon Bleu—and it wasn't bad! I also recall when a tray fell onto the dirty aft galley floor and a senior flight attendant blew the dirt off the lettuce leaves and tomatoes saying, "Hell, we have four hours to go; you don't want to upset any of those passengers. We are already short five meals!" Airlines have since made major changes by offering better food like yogurt, fresh fruit and healthy sandwiches.

Don't fly on an empty stomach. Eat a light meal and stay hydrated. Remember to eat before you board, bring a snack or bring enough cash to buy a snack onboard the airplane. You can check on the food service when you book your flight.

Onboard Lavatories

The type of aircraft will determine the number of lavatories. As there are a limited number of lavatories, you should try to use the airport restroom prior to boarding your plane. There are usually two lavatories in the back of the plane and one in the front which is for first class passengers and the cockpit crew. In most cases, due to security reasons, the first class lavatories are off-limits to the other passengers. The TSA discourages lavatory lines forming on an aircraft, especially outside the first class bathroom, as it is close to the cockpit. Also, due to safety regulations passengers are not permitted out of their seats during the last thirty minutes of a flight. So use the facilities early.

The waste tanks are emptied between every flight. There have been instances when one or more toilets blocked up in-flight and had to be closed off. The wait can become long at times!

Emergency Oxygen System

Individual oxygen masks connected to a central oxygen generator are stored in compartments above the passenger seats. Rows of seats usually have an extra mask (i.e., two seats, three masks) in case someone has an infant on his or her lap or someone in the aisle needs one. In the unlikely event that there is a problem with the cabin pressure where the level of oxygen in the cabin drops below a safe level, the masks will drop from the overhead compartment. The majority of commercial aircraft are pressurized at a maximum cabin altitude equivalent to 7,000 feet, where it is possible to breathe without an oxygen mask. If the cabin pressurization level reaches the equivalent of 14,000 feet or higher on the exterior or if there is a decompression above this flying level and hypoxia (a medical condition where the body is deprived of oxygen) develops, the compartments containing the oxygen masks will open automatically, either above or in front of the passenger and crew seats, and the yellow masks will drop. There are times, especially during extreme turbulence or a rough landing, when the compartment doors may loosen and the oxygen masks will drop. But don't panic. Follow the instructions given by the cabin crew.

In aircraft that fly above 14,000 feet, the FAA requires planes to carry onboard supplemental oxygen. At 18,000 feet, the atmospheric pressure is half that at sea level, decreasing further with altitude. This is why airplanes are pressurized to maintain a normal breathing atmosphere. When an aircraft is at 35,000 feet, you will feel like you are at only 7,000 feet.

There are small tanks of portable oxygen onboard that are used by the flight attendants in the unlikely event of an emergency, so that they can walk around the cabin as needed. They are also used as emergency medical oxygen for ill passengers.

Every aircraft has multiple pressurization systems: one or two automatic, a standby and a manual backup. The cockpit crew could descend the plane in a slow depressurization prior to supplemental oxygen being needed. Aircraft are required to be built so the fuselage could sustain a twenty-square-foot hole and remain flying. Most manufacturers increase the figure to forty square feet. In the unlikely event of an explosive depressurization, cabin pressure would equalize with the outside pressure almost instantly.

Seven Steps to Take in an OXYGEN Emergency

1. **O**xygen masks drop. Stay calm.
2. e**X**tend rubber tubing, put mask over face and breathe.
3. **Y**ield to instructions by the crew.
4. **G**et your mask on first and then assist your child or elderly passengers next to you.
5. **E**yes and ears alert to the crew and surroundings.
6. **N**ever panic.

Emergency Exits

The emergency exits are signified by a bright red exit light. Newer aircraft also have emergency path lighting or track lighting on the floor. There are white lights on the floor along the aisle, extending the length of the cabin, which become red at or near the exits of most planes. Your head should not be above the level of the seat armrests in the unlikely event of the plane filling up with smoke, because smoke rises. Always pay attention to the nearest exit when you get seated and count the rows of seats to the nearest exit when you board the plane. Make sure you familiarize yourself with your surroundings.

What to Do in an Emergency Evacuation

Boeing's literature instructs that in the event you experience an evacuation, you should:

- Try to remain calm.
- Listen to and follow instructions from the flight crew.

- Check to see if the closest exit is behind you.
- Leave your carry-on items aboard the airplane.
- Wear sturdy, comfortable shoes when flying.

Airplanes have numerous features to help facilitate a speedy evacuation:

- Escape path lighting will help passengers find their way to the exits in low-visibility conditions.
- Slides will deploy from each of the exits so passengers can get safely to the ground.
- If the airplane is in water, the slides can be used as life rafts. Seat cushions also double as flotation devices. They are easily removed and carried in an emergency.
- Airplanes used on oceanic routes also have inflatable life rafts onboard and a life vest under each seat.

Flotation Devices

Passenger airplanes are required to carry life rafts capable of containing all airplane occupants. Flotation equipment is required onboard all flights over water. Also, for each life raft, the airline must carry a survival kit that contains: radar reflectors, bailing water bucket, life raft repair kit, signaling whistle, canopy for sun shade, signal mirror, knife, carbon dioxide bottle for inflation, inflation pump, two oars, rope, magnetic compass, dye marker, flashlight with "D" batteries, at least one pyrotechnic signaling device, signaling flares, first aid kit, sea anchor to slow the drift of the raft, two-day supply of food with 1,000 calories for each occupant, candy snacks for strength and energy, sea water kit or water for each occupant, seasickness pills, fishing kit and a book on survival for the area of the airplane's route.

Every seat has its own life preserver located beneath it and most seats can be used as life preserver devices. Passenger life preservers are yellow and the crew members' are orange. A life preserver with a locator light is required for every occupant of the plane. The water-activated light illuminates automatically, is attached to the life preserver's shoulder and will work for up to ten hours. By pulling a lanyard, you inflate the vest by activating a compressed air cylinder. If this fails, there are manual inflation tubes to blow into. The flotation device must be located within the reach of the passenger and readily removable. Again, it is important to place your own life vest on first, then assist others.

Airlines are subject to the Federal Aviation Act. Regulations for emergency flotation devices require airplanes that are able to carry twenty passengers or more or have a maximum load of 6,000 pounds or more to follow the aforementioned regulations.

Escape Slides

Escape slides are built into the doors of the airplane and are used in the unlikely event of an evacuation. Depending on the size of the aircraft, an escape slide will open and inflate within three to five seconds. If a slide fails to inflate automatically, it can be activated manually by pulling a well-labeled lanyard. Slides on the newer airplanes double as rafts for emergency water ditching.

Fire Safety Equipment

There is fire safety equipment onboard each aircraft. The galleys are equipped with a traditional fire extinguisher as well as a water and antifreeze mix pressurized with carbon dioxide, which is stored in a green bottle. This type of extinguisher is used for paper-type fires.

Stored in a red container are the Halon fire extinguishers. These are more commonly used now and are the most adaptable pressurized liquefied gas extinguishers. There are at least two on each aircraft. Halon fire extinguishers can be used on all types of fires: grease, fuel, electrical and paper. In the past, the main concern was passengers smoking, but today smoking is prohibited on all airplanes. When smoking was permitted, a few back rows of the plane were considered the smoking section. But, as you can imagine, the smoke could be picked up throughout the entire cabin. For safety reasons, it was wise to prohibit smoking onboard an aircraft.

In the United States, the FAA sets the minimum safety requirements for each type of aircraft. All aircraft have emergency exits, emergency PA systems, supplemental oxygen systems, emergency lighting, life rafts and other flotation devices, fire extinguishers, etc. The only difference is that the capacity of each aircraft dictates the number of pieces of equipment.

First Aid Kit

The majority of U.S. airlines carry the medical equipment currently required by the FAA: one to four first aid kits depending on the number of passengers and one medical kit per aircraft. The first aid equipment is checked and restocked prior to each departure. The medical kit is stored in the cockpit. The first aid kits are found throughout the cabin. An FAA rule requiring most commercial airplanes to have AEDs (automated external defibrillators, which use electric shock to restore heart functions) went into effect in 2004. Most commercial airplanes must have cardiac equipment onboard. The FAA found that there were 119 cardiac-related events onboard aircraft, resulting in sixty-four deaths, between mid-1998 and mid-1999. During that period, automatic defibrillators were used seventeen times, saving four lives.[2]

First Aid Kit Contents

Each first aid kit must be accessible to the flight attendants and include:

- bandages
- compresses for applying pressure, moisture, heat or cold
- antiseptic swabs
- arm and leg splints
- tape
- scissors

Medical Kit Contents

An airplane's medical kit must be accessible to the flight crew, but can only be used by medical professionals. It includes:

- blood pressure cuff
- stethoscope
- plastic airways to deliver oxygen to help with breathing
- nitroglycerin tablets for chest pain
- dextrose solution for hypoglycemia

- epinephrine for asthma or allergic reactions
- injectable diphenhydramine HCl for serious allergic reactions
- hypodermic needles
- protective latex gloves
- sedatives, diuretics and other medications

Emergency Lighting

Since smoke rises and can obscure overhead lighting, the FAA determined that floor lighting could improve the evacuation rate by 20 percent under certain conditions. Some airlines now have yellowish, photo-luminescent lighting strips on the ceiling. They are charged before the first flight of the day by turning all the cabin lights to full bright. They are more reliable, because they require no battery power to operate.

Cabin Lighting

Cabin lights usually are adjusted to be bright for day flights, but the crew can set them as they see fit. In the evening, cabin lights are dimmed to help the eyes acclimate to outside conditions in an unlikely emergency situation. Once airborne, cabin lights are adjusted comfortably. Whenever cabin lights are adjusted during night flights, an announcement must be made informing passengers of the reading lights which are available in their customer service units. Lights will be adjusted for late night flights or when most of the passengers are sleeping.

PA System

The Passenger Announcement System is the system through which you get all announcements from the cabin crew and cockpit crew. A PA system is required anytime an aircraft is certified to carry more than nineteen passengers. If power fails, this unit is powered by backup batteries. It is a critical system for safety. It is important that you pay attention to all passenger announcements.

Emergency briefings on the PA

- ➢ Operation of your seat belt
- ➢ Location of all exits

- Review of the safety information card found in the seat pocket in front of you
- Smoking regulations
- Referencing the seat bottom cushions as flotation devices (life vests and rafts if flying over water) and referring you to the diagrams on the safety information card instructions on how to use them
- Making sure that the exit seating regulations are followed
- Instructions on use of oxygen masks in the unlikely event of a decompression

List the Equipment on the Plane

This exercise will help you to remember the airplane's equipment, so that you can have a comfortable and safe flight.

____________________ ____________________

____________________ ____________________

____________________ ____________________

____________________ ____________________

____________________ ____________________

____________________ ____________________

____________________ ____________________

____________________ ____________________

____________________ ____________________

____________________ ____________________

____________________ ____________________

____________________ ____________________

Points to Remember

My clients have felt it important not only to have a thorough understanding of the aircraft, but also to know what to expect during air travel. Knowing how the parts of the plane work tends to put your anxieties at ease.

Now you know what to do to help you experience a safe and comfortable flight! Remember:

- Pay attention to the flight attendants.
- Listen to the safety briefings, even if you've heard them before.
- Review the safety data card in the seat pocket in front of you.
- Locate the emergency exits, especially the one closest to you. Because airplanes have different configurations, look around you once you're in your seat.
- Count the number of rows between your seat and the closest exit; sometimes the nearest exit is behind you.
- Keep your seat belt fastened while seated. Turbulence can surprise you.
- When traveling with an infant or child under age two, consider purchasing a separate seat.
- Buckle your child into an approved-for-flying car seat.
- On longer flights, exercise your arms and legs.

Key Questions

1. What can vibrations and humming sounds come from?
2. When should you wear your seat belt?
3. What did you learn about airplane structure that has eased your mind?

chapter 9

Stories of Fear and Resolution

chapter goals:

To explore examples of several individuals who share the fear of flying, reminding you that you are not alone.

To show you how this book is effective for flying free of fear.

The following stories are based on real people who have successfully used my fear of flying program. In my practice, I've found that it helps to hear others' stories. Take a deep breath in and exhale all negative thoughts.

Thomas's Story

One dark and rainy spring day, Thomas's house was full of laughter, singing and talking, while several pieces of luggage sat by the large double front doors of the house. A female voice called out with excitement, "The limo is here! Grab your bags; we're off to the beaches of Hawaii." Oh, the thoughts of the white sandy beaches, tropical breezes, cascading waterfalls, sweet fragrances, brightly colored flowers and rich and varied cuisine of the islands. Samantha, a cool and bright sixteen-year-old, and her sister Michelle, a happy, eager ten-year-old, ran out of the house and into the blowing wind and heavy, beating raindrops. The familiar female voice once again called out, "Honey, let's go. The bags are in the limo!" Thomas's wife Trisha ran out to join the girls in the long, white car. Thomas slowly put on his hood and crept carefully toward the limousine, glaring at the airplane logo on the front passenger door. To the airport the stretch limo went. After a short thirty minutes, the limo pulled up to its airline's departing flights entrance.

The girls could not help staring at all the activity: passengers and visitors coming and going, flight crews walking through the terminal, pulling their luggage on wheelies, looking so professional and neat. Trisha, Samantha and Michelle couldn't refrain from talking, stopping only occasionally to catch their breath. As the three looked out the windows, they talked excitedly as they saw the jumbo jet pull into the terminal. Over the PA came the announcement the girls had eagerly awaited: "We will now begin boarding flight 214 to Hawaii. Those traveling with children or needing assistance may board at this time." Trisha called out to Thomas, "Honey, it won't be long now!" as she smiled into his large, dark eyes. After several rows were called, Samantha and Michelle yelled out, "That's us! Let's go, Dad!" When the three girls turned around with their eager, ecstatic faces to get Dad, they found only an empty seat and a torn-up tissue. Voices of dismay yelled out, competing with the final boarding call. *Where was Thomas?*

The plane took off and later landed in Hawaii, with its luxury hotels, palms and lagoon-pool complexes. Unfortunately, Trisha, Samantha, Michelle and Thomas were not onboard the flight!

Phillip's Story

One bitter cold, snowy February afternoon, around a large oval conference table, sat six businessmen at a high-powered corporation. The CEO proudly announced, "Gentlemen, to close this five-million-dollar deal, three of you will fly to Los Angeles on the six o'clock flight this evening. It will be worth the trip." The senior executive pulled out three airplane tickets. David, an employee of fourteen years, said after being handed a ticket, "Great, a vacation while my wife plays bridge with her friends." William, an employee of five years, responded after receiving the second ticket, "My wife isn't going to like this, but sunny California sounds good to me!"

Phillip, a young, new executive of two months thought, *I suppose those with more seniority will go, right? I won't be the other one, right?* The CEO stated in a gentle voice, "That's it, gentlemen; let's wrap up this deal," as he handed Phillip the third ticket. Phillip was unable to voice a response.

Walking to their cars, David and William said to Phillip, "Do you realize the bonus we will get when we return? This job has its rewards!" Phillip sighed as he drove home to pack.

A few hours later, the men arrived at the airport and boarded the plane to sunny California. David and William celebrated, thinking about the money they would receive and expressing hope that the plane would soon be taking off. Phillip suddenly darted out of his seat, announcing to his two colleagues that he forgot something and would return. He escaped down the center aisle, exiting the plane just as the last passenger entered the forward galley door. David and William waited for Phillip to return, but time ran out and the flight attendant then closed and armed the door to prepare for takeoff. The plane taxied to the runway and departed. David and William received their attractive bonuses while Phillip got a pink slip.

Jerry and Jen's Story

Jerry and Jen had a storybook wedding. The sparkling white snow glistened like fresh-cut diamonds outside the country club's tall windows. Voices expressed admiration for the happy newlyweds as they danced across the ballroom floor; Jerry in his tails and Jen in her satin gown trimmed with snow-white fur. The sparkling champagne glasses lifted and the toast was made, "To the new lovebirds. In a few hours you'll be flying off to the warm and luxurious British Virgin Islands; can you fit us in your luggage? Yes, the British Virgin Islands, where the lush tropical terrain meets the sea. Tennis courts, spas, pristine beaches, sailing, snorkeling and romantic candlelight dinners together on your patio, facing the yacht harbor, looking out at the moon and star-lit sea. We know you deserve such a magical place, just as you both deserve each other!"

Jen was blissful, counting the minutes down until Jerry would sweep her off her feet to begin the most memorable time of their lives. As she looked at her new husband, she whispered, "In three hours the flight attendant will be announcing, 'Fasten your seat belts.' Then off we go to paradise!" Jerry excused himself from his new bride and dashed to the rest room.

After the couple said their goodbyes to their guests and family, they changed their clothes, grabbed their bags and went to the airport. Jen looked excitedly into her new husband's wide eyes and said,

"Honey, this is going to be a honeymoon we will never, ever forget!" Well, it certainly was never forgotten.

While awaiting the boarding announcement, Jerry began to look a bit pale. Jen asked, "Honey, are you okay?" Jerry, the proud, dashing, new husband and man of her dreams replied, "Sure!" Jerry felt a lump in his throat, his stomach churning, his hands becoming cold and clammy, his mouth dry, his heart racing and his head somewhat dizzy.

A voice came over the PA: "We are now boarding flight 163 to the British Virgin Islands..." Jerry whispered in his bride's ear, "I'll be back," then rushed to the restroom.

The $10,000 honeymoon Jerry had saved up for to surprise his bride was lost. Jen waved goodbye to the plane as tears trickled down her flushed, warm cheeks, awaiting the arrival of her parents to take her home. Jerry could not be found, at least not at the airport.

Tiffany's Story

Tiffany was a forty-year-old mother of two: eight-year-old Brian and fifteen-year-old Cindy. Today was the last day of school and Tiffany's husband came home early from work. "Hey gang, everyone in the living room." Brian and Cindy ran down the stairs. Tiffany put down the box of rigatoni that she was just about to pour into a pot of boiling water and walked into the living room.

"Well, using my mega-money credit card has paid off. How would you like to spend a week in Orlando, Florida? We're going to Disney World!"

"Yeah! Hurray!" The family was screaming so loudly with joy, they could hardly hear each other's comments. Perhaps the most important comment of all was that from Tiffany:

"I have always wanted to drive through the southern states," she said.

"What, honey?" her husband asked. "Did you say drive? We get to fly! All those extra days we would have wasted driving will be spent at Disney's Magic Kingdom, Epcot Center, SeaWorld and one of the top golf resorts in America. What are we waiting for? Let's get packed!"

Tiffany sat down on the sofa with butterflies in her stomach. Was it the excitement of a fun family vacation to see Mickey and relax at the spa, with the beautiful beaches and the marina filled with sailboats?

Or were the butterflies from a feeling called fear? *Fear of what?* she asked herself. *I took a flight five years ago, to California; eight years ago, to Texas; I remember my white knuckles and the turbulence I felt when we flew through that awful thunderstorm.*

Tiffany knew she couldn't let her family down and looked forward to a vacation at a world-class resort. Three days before their wonderful vacation, Tiffany had trouble sleeping, difficulty eating and made several visits to the bathroom. The day arrived and Tiffany found herself wishing her family a fantastic time while she remained home to enjoy quiet time and catch up on some reading. Her children didn't quite understand why their mom wouldn't want to share this time with them, but they felt she deserved the vacation she said she needed. Tiffany's husband felt hurt but respected his wife's request.

Tiffany was too ashamed to tell her family that she was afraid to fly. This was the longest, loneliest, most tearful week Tiffany had ever experienced in her life. She felt like she let her family, and most of all, herself down!

Can You Relate to These Fearful Flyers?

I have listened to many stories like these during the years I've spent working with fearful flyers and I have empathized with each person involved.

There is so much that a person can miss out on when fear stands in his or her way. As you can see, the fear was very real to those affected by it, to the point of allowing it to paralyze them and interfere with their quality of life. If you allow fear to lead your life, it will! My question is: Why would anyone give fear permission to take over his or her freedom to enjoy life to its fullest?

Fear can cheat you out of special moments, time with family, enjoyable events and, above all, the opportunities of a lifetime.

"What Ifs?" are not allowed! I know you're leaning in that direction. We will discuss the nature of this problem presently.

Even though these four stories ended in disappointment, the good news is that these people all worked with me and now fly free of fear. I have received postcards from their various vacations and it is nice to know that the program has helped them and their families to enjoy life as it should be!

It helps to talk yourself into believing that you can fly free of fear. Try this exercise and repeat it often.

The Four I's

To fly fear free, keep repeating the four I's:

I can. • I will. • I am. • I do.

Doing this exercise will help you to condition yourself with positive thinking and familiarize your psyche and body with the notion that flying is normal. Let's go; yell out "The Four I's!"

Points to Remember

After hearing these stories, you can see that there are many other people who share your fear of flying. Let's review them and the impact that these fears had on their lives:

Thomas's Story: After the three girls turned around with their eager, ecstatic faces to get Dad, Thomas's seat was empty; only a torn up tissue was to be found. The family vacation, on the sunny beaches of Hawaii, was now an empty dream.

Phillip's Story: The plane taxied to the runway and departed, while Phillip never returned. David and William received their attractive bonuses, while Phillip got a pink slip.

Jerry and Jen's Story: Jen waved goodbye to the plane as tears trickled down her cheeks, awaiting the arrival of her parents to take her home. Jerry could not be found. Well, at least not at the airport. What a way to spend your honeymoon!

Tiffany's Story: Three days before their planned vacation, Tiffany had trouble sleeping, had difficulty eating and made several visits to the bathroom. Her children didn't quite understand why their mom wouldn't want to share time with them. Tiffany's husband felt hurt but respected his wife's request, as he and the children left Mom behind.

Key Questions

1. Whose story can you relate to: Thomas, Phillip, Jerry and Jen or Tiffany and her family? Why?
2. How do you think these fearful flyers overcame their fears?
3. How has a fear of flying affected *your* life?

PART III

Techniques for Flying Fear Free

chapter 10

Preparing for a Successful Flight

chapter goals:

To teach you how to develop your own flight plan, from making a reservation to the return flight and all the important steps in between.

To keep the development of your flight plan quick and easy without added stress.

To take away pressure for a more relaxed and successful flight.

Planning a flight can be stressful for anyone, but it is particularly stressful for a fearful flyer. Preparedness lowers your anxiety, which can help keep fear away. It begins with making the reservation, finding out the flight's length, time of departure and the type of aircraft, choosing your seat and meal, along with choosing your support person while giving them plenty of notice. This is a quick but helpful reminder chapter, so you don't need to wear a reminder string around your little finger.

Making the Reservation

It helps to book reservations far in advance if you can. Airlines release their seating anywhere from six months to eleven months prior to the flight. You might be able to save $100.00 or more if you book eight to ten months in advance. Fares change regularly based on availability, sales, etc. For some destinations, the cheapest fares can be had right before the flight, while with popular destinations or holidays, the lowest fares can sell out up to a year in advance. Most of the best standard fares need to be purchased three weeks in advance. You may be fortunate to purchase a cheap ticket on a massively under-booked flight a few days prior to departure. But if you need to be someplace by a certain date, it is not advisable to wait. If you need to purchase a ticket in a short period of time, you will most likely be paying top dollar.

Airline Ticket Sites

Here are some sites which offer great low-cost tickets where you can compare airline flights and prices. Survey these sites to find the perfect flight: Orbitz.com, priceline.com, Hotwire.com, Expedia.com, Travelocity.com, OneTravel.com, KAYAK.com, bookingbuddy.com, travel-ticker.com, CheapTickets.com, CheapAir.com, Mobissimo.com, Farecompare.com and StudentUniverse.com. You can also search "cheap airline tickets" or "airline tickets to (destination)" with any search engine. Or you can book directly through an airline's website.

Getting an Airline Ticket

➢ An **electronic ticket** (commonly abbreviated as **e-ticket**) is a digital ticket issued by an airline, replacing the older multi-layered paper tickets. Once your reservation is made, an e-ticket exists only as a digital record with the airline. You can print out your e-ticket, which contains:

- Official ticket number (including the airline's three-digit code)
- Terms and conditions
- Fare and tax details or "fare basis" code
- Fare restrictions
- Form of payment
- Issuing office
- Baggage allowance

➢ When **checking in with an e-ticket,** you will go to the ticket counter; it is not necessary to have the e-ticket with you. As long as you have your passport or credit card, the information can be retrieved from the airline's computer. Your reservation is based on your identity. You will then check in any luggage you are not taking as a carry-on. The e-ticket is not a substitute for your boarding pass, which must still be issued at the end of the check-in process.

- E-ticketing allows **different options** for checking in:
  - Online, telephone or self-service kiosk check-in (if the option is available)
  - Early check-in
  - Printing boarding passes at airport kiosks and at locations other than the airport
  - Delivering boarding pass barcodes via SMS or e-mail to a mobile device

The Length of the Flight

You may want to take the shortest flight or one with fewer stops or a non-stop, if available. You can explore the alternatives while choosing the best flight and see what works for you. Sometimes you have few options, but you will be fine whether you have stops along the way or not. Until you are comfortable, take short flights (forty-five minutes to one hour). Fly on Saturday (fewer people; the heaviest days of travel are Sunday afternoon, Monday and Friday). If you call the airline, you can discuss any questions you may have with the agent.

Choosing the Time of Your Flight

Depending on when you prefer to travel and the availability of flights, you can choose what time of day you wish to book. The early hour flights are usually the cheapest. You can check online to see what works best for you. If you fly at night, you can relax and get some sleep with a progressive muscle relaxation exercise, blanket and pillow.

On morning flights, you can still sleep or you can use any of your exercises and relaxation techniques: coloring, visualizing a picture, journaling, etc. During the day you can use your exercises and techniques, but you may want to listen to music or watch the in-flight movie, if it is offered. Some individuals prefer daytime so that they can watch the ground. Some prefer the night because the darkness makes one less aware of the altitude. Most of the flight, you can't see much on the ground anyway.

Selecting Your Seat

If you prefer more room and can afford the higher fee, booking in first or business class is recommended. First class costs two to seven times the coach class fare, depending on the length of the trip. Business class usually costs two to four times as much as coach class and affords you more room, more comfortable seats and better service. Both first and business class are in the front of the plane and quieter. Those who have claustrophobia can fly in moderate comfort in first and business class, given the extra space. Also, those who suffer from panic attacks feel less trapped in business and first class.

Coach class has some seating areas that can be considered, like the bulkhead row. This is the row of seats behind first class, just behind the partition that separates coach from first class. However, looking at a wall can be uncomfortable for some. Aisle seats are good, because you feel less confined. If you are afraid of heights, window seats are better because the plastic shade can be lowered, except for certain times such as landing and takeoff. Another area is the exit row: the seats beside the emergency exits. Remember, the seats in the emergency exit row do not recline and you could be required to perform in the unlikely event of an emergency. Would you prefer a window seat, so you can rest your head and look out or an aisle seat to stretch your legs? If you're fortunate not to have anyone sitting beside you, push up the armrests and get more comfortable. Just make sure your seat belt is on. If you have a blanket on, remember to buckle it over the blanket if you plan to sleep so the flight attendant doesn't have to disturb you to make sure your seat belt is fastened.

Ordering Your Meal (If Offered)

When you make a reservation for a longer flight that provides a meal, you can request a special meal such as a vegetarian, kosher or diabetic dish. Changes are being made regularly by the airlines, so always ask. In coach class, if the airline is offering food, it most likely must be purchased, although in first class on most airlines the food is still included in the ticket price. Make sure you bring your Goodie Bag (see chapter 17) and pack it with not only your helpful items, but also healthful snacks!

Finding Your Support Person

Many of my clients ask if they should have a support person with them and some won't fly without one. If you want a support person, choose someone who will be supportive regardless of your behavior or in-flight activities, such as making a "raisin face." Your support person can enjoy your accomplishment with you and have fun with your in-flight activities. It can help if he or she sits in on a relaxation session while on the ground, so he or she knows what to expect and can perhaps be helpful. He or she may want to experience the benefits of flying more comfortably.

My Preparation Checklist

This exercise will help you prepare for your flight by determining what is important to you, so that your stress level can be lowered and your flight made more enjoyable and affordable! Take time and rate each phase of preparation for your flight by checking the appropriate box in each row.

Rating Scale: 5: Primary Importance
4: Above Average Importance
3: Average Importance
2: Minor Importance
1: Very Little Importance

	5	4	3	2	1
Making My Reservation					
Airline Ticket Sites					
Length of the Flight					
Day or Night Flight					
Type of Plane					
Choosing My Seat					
Ordering a Meal (longer flight)					
Choosing My Support Person					

Next, make notes and put them in order, starting with the most important. For those with the same rating, place in the order of their importance on the same line. You may rate them all a five and use the information in the book to help you prepare for your flight.

1. ______________________________
2. ______________________________
3. ______________________________
4. ______________________________
5. ______________________________

Points to Remember

Preparedness lowers your anxiety, which can help keep fear away. Give yourself time to make reservations, check the length of the flight, select your seat, see if there's a meal, review airline regulations and choose a support person, if you feel you need one. You can find the information you'll need for your flight online, but if you have questions, don't hesitate to call the airline and ask. You may not have an option to choose the type of plane on which you would like to fly, but regardless of its type, remember, "I can and I will!"

Key Questions

1. What can you do to find the answers to your question(s)?
2. How prepared do you feel right now to take air travel?
3. How will you reserve your next flight?

chapter 11

Managing Fear and Building Courage

chapter goals:

To revisit the definition of fear and discuss how you can manage it.

To use exercises that practice building courage and removing fear to allow for a successful flight.

Managing fear means managing to the point of caution. Take pride in yourself for being cautious. Caution is a good thing and will keep you alert. Being totally fearless is unwise.

How does fear affect you?

Physical symptoms of fear that you may have experienced:

- Muscle tension, tremors (e.g., shaking hands)
- Loss of muscle control (e.g., weak knees)
- Inability to speak due to fear
- Heavy, labored breathing or difficulty breathing, shortness of breath not due to a heart problem or other medical condition
- Heart palpitations, chest pain or tightness not due to a heart problem or other medical condition
- Abdominal and intestinal discomfort, nausea, vomiting or diarrhea
- Inability to control bladder and bowels
- Sweating, weakness, dizziness, flushed or pale face, dry mouth, prickly or numb sensations

Psychological symptoms of fear that you may have experienced:

- Difficulty concentrating
- Poor cognition
- Impaired memory
- Narrowed perceptions
- Negative expectations
- Poor or fogged judgment
- Short temper
- Irrational thinking
- Random thoughts

Six Strategies for Managing Fear

1. Be vigilant.
2. Manage your information.
3. Control your mental images.
4. Focus on what you can control.
5. Establish routines.
6. Practice your stress management exercises and techniques.

Remember that fear is stimulated by information and misinformation:

- Make sure to confirm information and check for accuracy.

Control your mental images:

- Given the frequency of media information, concentrate elsewhere when possible.
    - ➢ Watch the news just long enough to get the story.
    - ➢ Focus on something enjoyable.

Types of information to avoid:

- Overgeneralizations
- Catastrophes
- Blaming

Usefulness of fear:

- Fear as a friend may be uncomfortable but valuable. Fear is like the "good pain" an athlete feels, not causing him or her to stop participating in an activity. The less you hate or fight the emotion, the easier it will be to live with.

Focus on what you can control:

- Fear is moderated by a sense of control.
- Make an intelligent plan for risk management.

Establish routines:

- A fear response is frequently a surprise.
- Anxiety is a dread of the next fearful surprise.
- Plan routines that incorporate emotionally rewarding experiences. Examples:
    - I always think of a peaceful place and walk through a guided imagery of it.
    - I talk to a friend or do an activity to keep my mind busy with positive thoughts.
    - Instead of dreading unwelcome surprises, I am consciously focusing on welcome routines.

Practice your stress management:

- Practice your breathing, guided imagery, progressive muscle relaxation and stretching exercises.
- Practice good healthy eating, drinking, sleeping and resting.
- Practice other techniques we discuss in this self-help book:
    - Color therapy
    - Music therapy
    - Coloring
    - Dreams
    - Cognitive-behavioral approaches

What is Courage?

Courage implies firmness of mind and will in the face of threat or complexity. It is almost never defined apart from its relation to fear. We think of courage as the characteristic of someone who acts despite fear (*Superman!*). Courage is the ability to "do the right thing" wisely regardless of feeling fear. Courage is really not a feeling; it is a way of acting. (Confidence is a feeling.) Nonetheless, when we experience ourselves being courageous, it seems like a feeling. We are aware that our hearts are engaged in some major way (the word *courage* comes from the Latin word for *heart*); we say we have (or do not have) the heart to do what needs to be done. It's a sense of strength that we find inside.

Practicing Courage

1. **Name something you are fearing or avoiding or some situation where you are lacking courage.**
   Example: I haven't been able to fly since Osama bin Laden's death. I am afraid of terrorist attacks.

   ____

2. **You have already said you are afraid. What consequence are you afraid of?**
   Example: I am afraid the plane will be hijacked and I may die.

   ____

3. **What is your fear like? What are its symptoms?**
   Example: Sweating, weakness in my knees, a queasy stomach.

   ____

4. **How can you use fear management tips to handle this emotion? Try using these tips to see if they help**:
   TIP ONE: Confirm information. Ask trusted sources for accurate information.
   Example: What can I find out about flight safety post-9/11?

   ____

   TIP TWO: Control mental images. For example, check the news for limited periods for information, but otherwise focus on other things.
   Example: Each time I rethink the images of planes crashing on 9/11, I will recall successful flights I and others have experienced and turn my attention back to where I want to be focused.

   ____

   TIP THREE: Establish routines. Remember that fear is unsettling; routines are grounding.
   Example: I'll buy my daughter and mother little gifts from my trip; they look forward to getting souvenirs and I like to give them. I'll call them before I get on the plane and spray on my lavender.

   ____

TIP FOUR: Practice your stress management. For example, be premeditated about your breathing, stretching, imagery, exercises, eating, drinking, resting (or sleeping).
Example: As soon as I get in my plane seat I'll immediately do my deep breathing exercises for five minutes and use my color chart.

____

5. **What goal do you want to accomplish while gaining courage?**
Example: Take reasonable precautions and fly in an airplane.

____

6. **List rational and intuitive pro and con arguments for your goal.**
Example:
Pros for taking air travel: *It's my job and I get to see a new part of the world.*
Cons for taking air travel: *It make me nervous and terrorists are still a threat.*
Pros for* not *taking air travel: *I'll be relaxed and I'll be less at risk.*
Cons for* not *taking air travel: *I won't get the promotion and the terrorists win.*
Your Pros and Cons list:
Pros for taking air travel: ______________________
Cons for taking air travel: ______________________
Pros for *not* taking air travel: ______________________
Cons for *not* taking air travel: ______________________

7. **Another approach to your decision is to do a cost/benefit analysis.**
Example:
Costs of taking air travel: *It makes me uncomfortable.*
Benefits of taking air travel: *I will increase my income and enjoy work more.*
Costs of* not *taking air travel: *I will jeopardize my job.*
Benefits of* not *taking air travel: *I would feel safer.*
Your Cost/Benefit Analysis:
Costs of taking air travel:

____

Benefits of taking air travel:

____

Costs of *not* taking air travel:

____

Benefits of *not* taking air travel:

____

8. **List the different paths you can take to less stressful air travel. Decide what seems the wisest; which is most in alignment with your values, goals and responsibilities?**
   Example:
   I could avoid certain heavy-traffic airports. This would be wise, because I want to take minimal risks.
   I could try to take only certain aircraft and limit how often I take air travel. This would be wise, because I only want to expose myself to risk for very good reasons.
   Your paths to safer, more relaxed air travel:

   ____

   ____

   ____

   ____

Points to Remember

Fear can be a disabler, but courage can manage your fear so that it is not disabling. To get over your fear of flying, it can be helpful to discover what is causing your fear.

You should now have an understanding of the physical symptoms associated with fear, such as muscle tension, perspiration, weakness and dizziness, and the psychological symptoms of difficulty concentrating, poor judgment, short temper and more. Now that you understand them, you can work on them! Next, you learned strategies for managing your fear, being proud to be cautious, managing your information, controlling your mental images, focusing on what is controllable and knowing what exercises and techniques to use so you can practice your routines.

Key Questions

1. What is fear? What is courage?
2. Why haven't you been able to face your fear of flying until now?
3. What is your confidence level as you begin to apply the strategies and techniques you are learning and move forward in this book?

chapter 12

Handling Anxiety

chapter goals:

To address anxiety and teach you a healthier approach for letting go of worry and fear.

To improve physically, mentally, emotionally and spiritually when dealing with stress.

To help ease your anxious mind, relieve your physical concerns and establish a healthy balance that will promote your upcoming flight.

Worry and fear can make you anxious if you allow them to, but you can take control and work on your problem. It is essential to understand the problem and how to improve physically, mentally, emotionally and spiritually.

Understanding Your Anxiety

Have you ever asked yourself, "Why can't I get on a plane?" or "Why can't I enjoy flying like the rest of them?" To understand yourself and your fear, you need to:

- Listen to your body signals. What are they telling you?
- Use positive feedback from others.
- Resist running from your problem; be honest with yourself.
- Discover what you can control and what you can't.
- Reject living in denial or negativity.

- Become aware of how you react to the situation.
- Be ready to work on the problem.
- Use what helps physically, mentally, emotionally and spiritually.
- Believe in yourself: "I can and I will!"

Behaviors that Suggest a Fear of Flying

- Inability to listen to conversations on the topic of airplanes or the airline industry
- Excessive use of alcohol or sedatives or changes in behavior prior to or during a flight
- A need to drive, when flying makes more sense
- Communication via telephone, fax, text message or e-mail when face-to-face contact is needed
- Avoidance of scheduling appointments that necessitate flying
- Discrepancy in job performance; e.g., unable or more difficult to attend trainings or conferences that require flying
- Missing family events due to avoidance of flying
- Sick or uncomfortable feeling when hearing or seeing an airplane or being at an airport
- Family problems due to not flying
- Losing a job or promotion due to the avoidance of flying

Developing a Healthy Attitude

One of the most important factors in life is your attitude. Attitudes are our evaluations of different aspects of the social world. When we observe someone who shares our attitudes and beliefs, it makes us feel good about ourselves, because it makes us feel normal and in touch with the world. But we must be realistic with our actions. That is why I recommend that you don't spend much time with those who share your fear of flying. Associate with only those who are positive regarding flying. It doesn't hurt to be around positive individuals. If you believe that you will fail to fly, then you will fail. This is known as a *self-fulfilling prophecy*.

The reason people compare themselves to others is to validate their own abilities and opinions. There is no accurate or objective means to evaluate one's self, so we depend on others' informative observations. Also, one might wonder why people adopt attitudes and behaviors from those they observe. Comparing ourselves to others helps us to determine if our view of reality is true or not. Individuals can change their attitudes to that of those close to their values and with those they can identify with. Also, one's concept of oneself can be a significant factor. Some people just want to feel good about themselves and by desiring to appear like a positive figure, one feels better about who he or she is.

You can develop a healthy attitude if you:

- Learn to accept what you cannot change and begin working on what you can (your fear of flying).
- Employ positive thinking.
- Are not so hard on yourself; realize you are human and not perfect.
- Accept yourself, love yourself and be patient with yourself.
- Live in the present, not in the past. Be consistent.

Changing Your Attitude

Step 1: Understanding Myself: What are my body signals? What can I control and what can I not?

____

____

____

____

Step 2: What is the effect of attitude on my behavior? (emotions and mood about flying)

____

____

____

____

Step 3: What will I do to develop a healthy attitude?

____

____

____

____

Controlling Your Emotions

It's okay to express your emotions, but you need to learn how to control them when needed!

- Ask yourself, "How do I feel?" Get in touch with your emotions.
- Learn how to let out your bottled-up emotions.
- Find someone who will listen and share your feelings.
- Don't keep your feelings locked up inside. If you can't talk about how you're feeling, write it out.
- Are your emotions realistic? Where are they coming from?

Easing Your Anxious Mind

- Stay in reality and utilize the information that you know.
- Relax.
- Don't blame yourself, don't feel that you are alone and remember you can overcome your anxiety and fear.
- Use positive self-talk: "I can and I will!"

Making Physical Improvements

Taking care of yourself physically is a major key to lowering your anxiety and stress level. I have seen individuals become ill due to worry and fear. Stress can take a toll on your health, so don't let it. Let's look at a few key points:

- Relax and employ the relaxation techniques you'll learn in this book.
- Maintain a regular sleep schedule.
- Follow a well-balanced diet. Don't skip meals. Leave out the caffeine, sugar, salt, fatty foods and alcohol!
- Decrease or eliminate nicotine use.
- Stay away from unnecessary drugs.

Tina's Story

Tina, a high school mathematics teacher, was in the teacher's lounge when she got drawn into a conversation with her colleagues regarding air travel. Tina was planning a trip with her husband to go visit his sister in France. Tina, who was a fearful flyer, was experiencing anxiety concerning the flight. She had been worrying and listening to her colleagues, especially one other teacher who shared in her fear. Her anxiety was building as she listened to the negative comments. Tina and the other teacher discussed a few of the bad experiences they had on past flights, from delays to lost baggage, etc. Of course, Tina tuned out the other teachers who were discussing the great experiences they had on past flights and trips. Because of her fear, anxiety and worry, Tina related to the teacher who shared her feelings.

Remember that when you observe or listen to someone who shares your attitudes and beliefs, it makes you feel good about yourself, because it makes you feel normal and in touch with the world. What should Tina have done? Definitely not team up with someone with a negative attitude. If Tina had listened to the other teachers' good experiences, it would have built her positive attitude toward flying. You feed off others. You don't want to be around negativity. Stay positive!

Individuals who are exposed to certain stimuli or events (such as a bad experience on a flight) will make the information held in memory more available, which is called *priming*. In most cases we use the stored information for the good, but unfortunately, we also store the negative. Turn negative thoughts into positive thoughts. This is where you have control over the situation. "You can and you will!"

Points to Remember

Worry and fear can have a hold on you if you allow them to, but you can take control and work on your problem! Establish a healthy balance in your lifestyle, so that you can work through your fear and stop the worrying. It isn't just about changes that involve flying; you need to make changes in your daily life which will not only lower your stress level but also help you to handle future stressful situations, such as flying on an airplane. You must keep a positive attitude and believe in yourself.

It's okay to let out your emotions but you need to learn how to control them when necessary. Don't blame yourself, don't feel that you are alone and remember you can overcome your anxiety and fear. Taking care of yourself physically is a major key to lowering your anxiety and stress level. One of the most important five-letter words that you need to keep in your mind is *relax*. Be ready to use the tools you have at your fingertips.

Key Questions

1. What four areas should you focus on to help yourself?
2. If you can't talk about your feelings, what can you do?
3. What is your anxiety management plan?

chapter 13

How Foods Affect Your Travel Experience

chapter goals:

To address the nutritional choices that can reduce your stress and anxiety before a flight.

To follow the list of foods that you should eat and learn which foods should be avoided.

Airports don't offer many healthful alternatives to the food you may be served onboard an airplane, but if you are watchful you may find some healthful foods offered in the terminal. If you are not traveling on a longer flight, you most likely will have to pay for what you eat in-flight, if food is even an option.

To remain healthy while flying, eat a healthful snack or meal before you fly and pack a healthful snack in your purse or carry-on. Also, keep in mind that breakfast is the most important meal of the day, so don't miss it.

Remember that carrying liquids is not permitted until you go through security. You can buy a beverage then or you can wait until you are onboard the plane and look for the beverage service cart to come by. Once your plane reaches cruising altitude and the captain informs the flight attendants, they will come through the cabin to offer you a hot or cold beverage or an alcoholic drink such as beer, wine or whiskey.

Good Snack Foods for Air Travel

- Granola bars
- Trail mix
- Whole grain crackers filled with peanut butter/cheese
- Fresh or dried fruit and cut-up fresh vegetables
- Nuts
- Cheese
- A sandwich wrap, if you eat it before it spoils
- Low salt pretzels
- Ginger snaps (treat for nausea)
- Candied ginger pieces
- Dry cereal
- Sugar-free gum (to keep your ears from popping)

What You Should Eat on an Airplane

A high carbohydrate diet is recommended; sometimes airline meals are high in fat and preservatives and low in carbohydrates and are not advisable. The low air pressure, high altitude environment causes all parts of our bodies to swell up, even our intestines. Salty foods should be avoided and you should choose a low sodium diet. A carbohydrate diet can help you function more effectively and think more clearly at higher altitudes. It can be helpful to bring your own food or order a special meal if possible, depending on your flight time and airline policy.

The special diets the airlines offer are relatively more appetizing and have less fat. You may be offered meals like:

- Steamed and sautéed vegetables
- Pasta
- Whole grain rice
- Salads
- Fresh raw vegetables
- Baked meats, poultry and fish
- Special sandwiches on specific breads (rye, wheat, whole grain)

Keep in mind that cooked foods are easier to digest!

Special Meals Some Airlines Offer

- **Vegetarian**
  - No meat, fish or eggs
  - Usually includes dairy products
- **Kosher**
  - Cutlery and plates have never been used before
  - Meat is slaughtered, cooked and served according to Kosher law
- **Hindu**
  - Spicy
  - Indian-style vegetarian
- **Muslim**
  - No pork
- **Child's Plate** (varies by airline and/or month)
  - Hamburger
  - Pizza
  - Hot dog
  - Grilled cheese
  - Spaghetti
  - Macaroni and cheese
  - Chicken fingers

Children usually enjoy the "Kids Meals" of airline food!

- **Fruit Plate**
  - It's usually fresh!
  - Ask the flight attendant to leave on the plastic wrap so that you may snack on it throughout your flight
  - You may request yogurt if it's available
- **Seafood**
  - Usually a choice between cold seafood salad or seafood entrée
  - You may request a sandwich if it's available

I've had passengers admit that they *always* order a special meal. Airlines may honor other dietary restrictions like diabetic, low calorie, low sodium, gluten free, lactose free and more—it's best to contact the airline directly.

Four Steps to Order a Special Meal

1. Request it when you make your reservations.
2. Reconfirm it with reservations forty-eight hours before departure.
3. Ask when you check in, "Is my special meal listed in the computer?"
4. Confirm with the flight attendant after boarding, prior to takeoff. At this time, you can give the flight attendant a note with your meal request/name/seat number.

Foods to Avoid:

Major Stimulants

- Alcohol
- Coffee and tea (herbal and non-caffeinated are okay)
- Cola (caffeine)
- Cigarettes
- High-sugar foods, candy or chocolate

Others

- Acid-producing foods
    - Certain fruits
    - Meats
    - Fish
    - Cheeses
- White flour
    - Wheat, rye, multi-grain and whole grain are okay.
- Fruit juices containing sugar
    - You can dilute with soda water or mineral water.
- Salty foods
    - Chips (Light or no-salt are okay.)
    - Pretzels (Light or no-salt are okay. Remember they help upset stomachs.)
- Fatty and greasy foods
    - Fast foods; hamburgers, French fries
- Gassy foods
    - Carbonated beverages
    - Beans
    - Cabbage

- Sweets
  - White sugar
  - Carbohydrates in refined form

Foods to Choose:

- Vegetables
- Fruit
- Nuts
- Seeds
- Ginger snaps/ginger
- Mints
- Plenty of water: While in-flight, drink water every hour. Cabin air is drier (0 to 2 percent humidity) than the desert. Alcohol, coffee and tea have diuretic effects, so drink extra water.
- Chamomile tea: This tea is a natural relaxant. Drink three to four cups throughout the flight, if it agrees with you.

Stay seated with your seat belt fastened low and snug, but get up and move around the cabin when you are permitted to. This is when you should use the restroom. Especially on long flights, movement prevents possible medical problems.

Foods That May Help Protect You from Radiation

Many individuals, especially fearful flyers, have been concerned regarding exposure to radiation when flying. This information is provided for educational purposes only:

- **Seaweed and other sea vegetables:**
  - **Kelp,** which has twelve milligrams of iodine per teaspoon of granules. Sprinkle it onto any meal.
  - **Kombu,** which is a type of kelp that comes in strips. (Add one five-inch strip to a pot of soup, grains and beans. Iodine is not affected by heat.
  - **Dulse and wakame** which are other good sources of iodine.
- **Vegetables:** asparagus, garlic, lima beans, mushrooms, soybeans, summer squash, onions, red bell peppers, beets, broccoli, Brussels sprouts, kale, spinach, watercress, Swiss chard, turnip greens

- **Seeds and nuts:** almonds, sunflower seeds, Brazil nuts, sesame seeds
- **Fruits:** Apples, papaya, strawberries, kiwis, guava, quince, plums, gooseberries, oranges, grapefruit, lemons, limes, pineapples, olives
- **Whole grains:** especially brown rice
- **Other:** miso soup, green and black tea, brewer's yeast/nutritional yeast, reishi and cordyceps mushrooms
- **Herbs:** rosemary, curcumin (turmeric), burdock root, cilantro leaf, eleuthero/Siberian ginseng, holy basil/tulsi aerial parts, milk thistle
- **Vitamins:** A, B Complex, C with bioflavonoids, D, E, K

Benefits of Omega-3s and Vitamins

Preparing for air travel can be stressful, especially if you are a fearful flyer. When your body is stressed, perhaps not rested, your resistance may be lower than usual and then you're put into a crowd where some people may be carrying colds along with their luggage. So, what can you do to help prevent from getting sick? Getting at least seven hours of rest is a start, along with eating a well-balanced diet high in Omega-3s, vitamins and antioxidants. Plus drinking plenty of water and taking a multivitamin boosts the immune system.

Foods with Omega-3s

Unsaturated fatty acids, Omega-3s can boost the immune system:

- Salmon
- Tuna
- Walnuts
- Ground flax
- Dried chia seeds
- Butternuts
- Spices (cloves)

Foods That Fight Colds and Flu

- Vitamin C: bell peppers (especially red), leafy greens, broccoli, kiwi fruit, citrus fruit, berries (especially blueberries)

- Vitamin A (especially good for your eyes): carrots, sweet potatoes, pumpkin, spinach, fish (cod, salmon, halibut)
- Tea (especially green tea which can enhance the immune system with a high concentration of polyphenols with anti-oxidants)

Relaxation Benefits of Tea

You should consult your physician before using herbal tea for anxiety. Only a qualified medical or psychological professional can diagnose and treat anxiety disorders. Tea should not take the place of prescribed medication; in most cases, it is looked to as a dietary aid, not a cure. The mind, body and soul can benefit from a soothing cup of tea; it puts you in a positive mood that helps you feel relaxed. More than twenty-three million Americans experience anxiety. Research conducted by the U.S. Food and Drug Administration and other health associations has concluded that some herbal teas contain a natural composition of several compounds that can affect the brain, heart and cognition positively.

Types of Tea and Their Benefits:

- **Anise Tea**: A sweet treat with soothing mucilage that eases dry, bronchial and asthmatic coughs, calms stomach, soothes digestion, eases flatulence and sweetens breath.
- **Black Tea**: A painkiller and sedative that helps soothe muscle and nerve pain, neuralgia, rheumatism and menses pain and provides menopause relief and hormone balance.
- **Blueberry Tea**: One of the healthiest foods and teas. Anti-oxidants help neutralize harmful by-products of metabolism known as free radicals that can lead to cancer and other age-related diseases. Like cranberry tea, it cleanses the urinary tract and prevents infections. Helps with eyesight, is an expectorant for coughs, cleanses the gastrointestinal tract, helps prevent heart disease and slows down the aging process.
- **Chai Tea**: A full antioxidant that boosts the immune system and prevents illness. It benefits from its spices: cardamom, cinnamon, cloves, ginger, nutmeg and pepper. Cardamom

relieves indigestion; cinnamon stimulates other herbs helping them for faster healing, lowers blood pressure, reduces pains and fevers and relieves indigestion, nausea, gas, heartburn, menstrual cramps; cloves relieve flu and colds and invigorate the body; ginger fights common colds and flu, strengthens and heals respiratory and digestive systems, cardiovascular, ulcers, and reduces fever and aches; nutmeg helps keep mucous membranes moist, especially in the throat; pepper helps stimulate taste buds, improves digestion, prevents gas, both antibacterial and antioxidant agents.

- **Chamomile Tea**: Tranquilizes, relaxes and soothes nerves, helps insomnia, relaxes muscles and softens skin. Helps with aches, pains, cramps, bladder infections and nausea.
- **Chocolate Mint Tea**: Lifts mood, gives energy, relaxes, reduces stress and enhances alertness and focus. Helps with digestion, colds, fatigue, heartburn, nausea, bad breath, headaches, stomach cramps, toothaches, body odor and palpitations.
- **Cinnamon Tea**: Sweet and calming, it helps colds, chills, arthritis and rheumatism. It stimulates other herbs, helping them for faster healing, lowers blood pressure, reduces pains and fevers and relieves indigestion, nausea, gas, heartburn and menstrual cramps.
- **Cranberry Tea**: Helps with urinary tract infections and contains vitamin C.
- **Ginger Tea**: Fights colds and flu. Helps with digestion, respiratory and digestive systems, nausea and motion sickness; fights arthritis, lowers cholesterol, stabilizes blood pressure and heart functions and soothes the stomach; a warming tea that motivates appetite and metabolic increase to burn calories. Helps ulcers, reduces fever and body aches. Caution: avoid if you have peptic ulcers.
- **Ginseng Tea**: Antioxidants to prevent cellular aging, raises HDL (good cholesterol), helps regulate blood sugar levels, deep-cleans tissues, stimulates production of red and white blood cells to fight disease. Helps fight impotence and frigidity.

Useful in fighting fatigue, exhaustion and depression from nervous disorders. Caution: Ginseng is a tonic to be avoided if there are inflammatory conditions, bronchitis, high blood pressure or if taking other stimulants.

- **Green Tea**: Its antioxidants help as an anticancer agent; it lowers cholesterol, helps metabolize fats, reduces blood pressure, regulates blood sugar and helps prevent cardiovascular disease. Fights colds, flu and viruses. High in fluoride for healthy teeth and gums, helps with diabetes, bone density, radiation poisoning, asthma, arthritis, skin problems, pancreatic and prostate cancer; anti-aging, anti-bacterial, anti-inflammatory and antiviral.
- **Lavender Tea**: Works on the brain, relieves stress, headaches, anxiety, depression, mood swings, dizziness and fainting. Reduces fevers, detoxifies the body. Can be used as a gargle for toothaches, sore throats and laryngitis, providing antiseptic protection to fight infections; eases vomiting and diarrhea, good for travel.
- **Licorice Tea**: Mood lifter for depression, aids concentration. Helps with indigestion, reduces stomach acid, allergies, and asthma. Caution: Avoid licorice if you have hypertension, heart problems, thyroid or kidney disorders. Glycyrrhizin in licorice can cause headaches, edema, heartburn and cardiac problems in high quantities.
- **Lemon Tea**: High in vitamin C and bioflavonoids to fight infections, prevents thickening of arterial walls, strengthens veins, blood vessels, capillaries; prevents bruising and varicose veins. It has vitamins A, B1, B2, B3 and mucilage. The antiseptic, antirheumatic, antibacterial, antioxidant agents reduce fevers and remove acid wastes from the body. Lemon in hot water with sugar or honey can be used for coughs and colds.
- **Marshmallow Tea**: Anti-inflammatory agent to speed up healing; an oxygenator helping to fight cellular aging, strengthens kidneys, muscle aches and pains, helps lower blood sugar levels, provides protein for vegetarians and muscle builders, eases throat inflammation and laryngitis.

- **Orange Tea**: Energy booster, aids digestion, reduces constipation and bloating, expectorant for phlegm, soothes nervous system, eases spasms, helps dissolve kidney stones, fights infection.
- **Peppermint and Spearmint Tea**: Instant energy, mood elevator, eases pain, headaches and tension. Reduces stress and helps with nausea and motion sickness. Helps concentration and alertness. Refreshes breath, helps with body odor. Helps relieve IBS (irritable bowel syndrome).
- **Parsley Tea**: Glands, liver and gallbladder cleanser and mild antibiotic to fight infections. It has B-complex, antioxidants, vitamins A and C, chlorophyll for cells, silicon for tissue repair, protein, and zinc. Helps with recovery from illness, natural antihistamine for asthma, allergies, hay fever and headaches.
- **Pineapple Tea**: Loaded with vitamins and minerals. Nutrients include calcium, potassium, fiber and a good source of vitamins A and C. Strengthens bones, rich in manganese; helps colds and coughs, loosens mucus.
- **Raspberry Tea**: Gargle with it for canker sores and bleeding gums. Helps diarrhea, tones lower body organs and pelvic muscles in women, urinary tract and kidney strengthening, has vitamins A, B-complex, C, E, citric and malic acids, niacin, iron, magnesium, pectin, potassium, selenium, silicon, sodium and zinc.
- **Vanilla Tea**: Calms sugar cravings, curbs appetite, elevates mood, used for sweetness.
- **Wild Strawberry Tea**: Helps soothe gastrointestinal inflammations and infections, digestive disorders and rheumatic gout. Good source of iron and vitamins to nourish and strengthen the body after surgery, cleanse the liver, used for recovery from hepatitis.
- **Honey in Tea**: Immediate energy booster, antibacterial agent, reduces muscle fatigue for athletes, great taste as sweetener, natural remedy for ailments and arthritis, immunity system builder, keeps levels of blood sugar fairly constant, a sobering agent, soothes throats, used in warm milk or chamomile tea for insomnia.

Packing a Snack

Prepare for your flight by choosing some of the healthful snack foods listed for the plane.

____

____

____

____

____

____

____

Points to Remember

To remain healthy when taking air travel, eat a healthful snack or meal before you fly and pack a healthful snack in your purse or carry-on. Also, keep in mind that breakfast is the most important meal of the day. There are some great snacks to pack such as granola bars, trail mix, whole grain crackers filled with peanut butter or cheese, dried fruit, etc. A high carbohydrate diet can help you function more effectively and think more clearly at higher altitudes. Salty foods should be avoided, as swelling and edema may occur when flying. If you need a special meal and there is food service on your flight, you may request it by following the airline's steps for special meals.

Foods to avoid that exacerbate anxiety are major stimulants like alcohol, caffeinated beverages, high-sugar foods like chocolate and other candy. Other foods to stay away from are acid-producing foods, sweets, white flour, fruit juices containing sugar and foods that are salty, fatty, greasy and gassy. Traveling can be stressful, especially air travel, so getting at least seven hours of rest and eating a well-balanced diet that is high in Omega-3s, vitamins and antioxidants can help prevent you from getting sick. Drinking plenty of water and taking a multivitamin helps too. Herbal teas can be beneficial and relaxing and it is helpful to know how different teas can affect your mood and your health. You can find tea that will not only help you for your needs, but also soothe and relax you!

Key Questions

1. Which foods will you bring with you for your next flight and which will you avoid?
2. What teas, if any, will you try?
3. How do tea and food affect your mood and health?

chapter 14

Benefits of Aromatherapy

chapter goal:

To discuss the holistic approach and the benefits of aromatherapy in combating anxiety prior to flights.

Today, many individuals are turning to healing practices beyond mainstream medicine. Aromatherapy utilizes the natural aromatic essences or oils extracted from wild or cultivated plants to treat illness, aid relaxation, promote health and soothe the body. Animals have always eaten certain herbs and grasses when they felt ill. Aromatherapy has been used for centuries. The oils are usually vaporized and inhaled or used as massage oils. The Mayo Clinic theorizes that compounds in the oils may activate specific parts of the brain, which then release brain chemicals which have relaxing effects.

An appropriate way to use aromatherapy onboard is to pack a sachet pouch. Take any of these herbs and scents and put them in a small pouch that you can keep in your carry-on or handbag. Every once in a while, pull out the pouch and let the scents relax you.

Let's take a closer look at some scents that are ideal for relieving air travel stress.

Scents That May Aid Relaxation

Lavender is a fragrant evergreen shrub native to southern Europe, especially around the Mediterranean. The majority of the commercial crop is grown in France, Spain, Bulgaria and Russia. Lavender is the oil most associated with burns and healing of the skin and is believed to cure headaches. Lavender is known to induce relaxation. Wherever lavender grows, the air is calmed and stress has a way of disappearing. Lavender is helpful for insomnia and jet lag. Used in the form of: plant, candles, bath oil, air spray, lotion, sachet, body splash/oil/spray/cologne.

COLOR: Cool. It helps you overcome negative feelings, calms you and reduces your anxiety level. Helpful to use with: clothing, wall paint, furniture, bedding, drapes, umbrellas, luggage, writing paper/envelopes, pens, tissues, dinner cups and dishes.

Basil is a strong aromatic herb that originated in India but is now grown in many countries around the Mediterranean, Morocco and Florida. This plant is often known as the royal herb, derived from the Latin word for "royal." Basil is good for the nervous system and is valuable for nervous fatigue, insomnia, mental and physical tiredness and jet lag. For stress, a mixture of one teaspoon soy oil, a drop of marjoram, and two drops of basil oil are rubbed all over the body. Basil is also effective for migraine relief, colds and sinus problems. For a soothing effect, infuse basil leaves in hot water and drink as an herbal tea. Used in the form of: tea, candles, plant, oil, body splash with mint, soups, sauces, etc.

COLOR: Cool. It balances energy. Helpful to use with: clothing, wall paint, furniture, bedding, drapes, writing paper/envelopes, pens, tissues, cups and tea pots.

Tangerine is a member of the orange family and originated in China. Tangerines grow in the Mediterranean regions of Europe and North Africa and in North and South America. They are very good for stress and irritability. If you are nervous and have insomnia, it would help to eat a few tangerines after dinner, in the evening. The bromine content, a substance sedative to the nervous system, is higher in mandarins and tangerines than in any other fruit. Drink its juice instead of orange juice; it is also rich in vitamin C. Although tangerine calms the nervous system, it can be energizing to your spirit. Used in the form of: juice, food, candy drops, oil/body splash/spray, detergent, air spray and lip gloss.

COLOR: Warm. Helpful to use with: clothing, wall paint, furniture, breakfast dishes and cups, color samples of material/paper to glance at for energy, lamp shades for kitchen, highlighters, etc.

Jasmine is a genus of two hundred species of tender and hardy deciduous and evergreen shrubs whose flowers have a beautiful fragrance. It originated in India, China and Persia. Egypt is the largest producer of Jasmine. Jasmine is a relaxing scent that offers sensuality and harmony. Jasmine tea is a green tea with jasmine blossoms, an antioxidant mix of delicate flavor. Used in the form of: oil, potpourri, candles, air spray, body spray/cologne/perfume, tea, etc.

COLOR: Warm. Helpful to use with: clothing, wall paint, furniture, jewelry, socks, gloves, etc.

Mint is made up of three chief species: spearmint, peppermint and pennyroyal. Mint is originally a native of the Mediterranean region, introduced into Britain by the Romans. The American Midwest is now an important producer of peppermint oil. Mint is a cognitive stimulator; it invigorates and alerts concentration. It is used medicinally and commercially. Peppermint calms sickness and nausea. Mint tea has been helpful for alleviating migraine headaches. In biblical times, mint was so valued it was used to pay taxes. Mint tea is used for instant energy. This plant eases pain, headaches and tension. It's a great tea to take in a thermos for long-distance drives or work. It reduces stress without putting you to sleep. Used in the form of: tea, plants, candles, candy, mints, oil, food, bath oil, medication flavoring, mouthwash and toothpaste flavoring, chewing gum, breath mints, etc.

COLOR: Cool. Helpful to use with: clothing, wall paint, furniture, bedding, drapes, cups, dishes, napkins, tissues, jewelry, food and drinks.

NOTE: Mint oil is very concentrated: one pound of mint oil can flavor 40,000 sticks of chewing gum or between 1,000 to 1,500 tubes of toothpaste.

Blueberry is the state berry of Maine and is also known as bilberry, whortleberry and hurtleberry. It is named after its velvety, deep-blue color. Europeans in North America gathered and dried the fruit for use in the winter. The blueberry is a member of the Ericaceae family, which includes rhododendron, azalea, Indian pipe, heath, cranberry and huckleberry. Blueberries have the best antioxidant activity out of forty commercially available fruits and vegetables. Research shows health benefits include: anti-aging, cancer prevention, urinary tract health and vision health. In Japan, wild blueberry has been named the "vision fruit." Used in the form of: candles, potpourri, sprays, foods, drinks, candy and lip gloss. You can eat them right from the bush or freezer, toss them into cereals or salads, add to waffles and muffins, smoothies, ice cream or yogurt and even make them into wine.

COLOR: Cool. Helpful to use with: clothing, wall paint, furniture, bedding, cups, dishes, writing paper, pens, jewelry, drapes, bathroom accessories, etc.

Make an Aromatherapy Worksheet

Use this exercise to find out which aromatherapy plants and scents are helpful for you. My clients have had fun with this exercise and you will, too. Test the scents and see how they make you feel. You can keep a library of your results for your future needs. Relax and take in the relaxing or energizing aromas.

Essential oils:

____

____

____

____

Plants:

____

____

____

____

Sprays/Splashes:

____

____

____

____

Additional Notes:

____

____

____

____

Points to Remember

Many individuals are turning to healing practices beyond mainstream medicine. Complementary and alternative therapies are becoming more and more popular. Along with different theories and techniques, professionals are finding that alternative therapies are proving to be effective for many sufferers of various disorders and illnesses, including fear of flying. Aromatherapy has been around much longer than many think and the term has been used since 1937. Aromatherapy is the practice that uses the oils of various plants to treat illness, help you relax, promote health and simply soothe the body. Lavender, basil, tangerine, jasmine, mint and blueberry are just a few helpful scents, especially for fear of flying. The exercise will help you discover which plants and scents may help you cope with your fear of flying.

Key Questions

1. What is aromatherapy?
2. Which scents will you use in your aromatherapy?
3. In what ways can you employ your favorite scents around the house and during air travel?

chapter 15

Using Color Therapy

chapter goals:

To explore the positive effects of using color therapy for fear of flying.

To show you how to design and implement your own collection of color cards for reducing anxiety during air travel or any other stressful situation.

To teach you exercises using colors for reducing stress, anxiety and panic.

With *color therapy* you can create any atmosphere that you desire, helping to relax you in many situations. Every day our moods and physical desires are affected without us ever realizing it. The next time you're at a fast-food restaurant, look around at the décor. The colors are bright, exciting and fun. Do you think the decorators picked those colors just so you would be cheerful while you're in their establishment? There's more to it than that: bright colors, such as red, orange, green and yellow, have been proven to stimulate the nervous system and increase your appetite. The color yellow is also known to improve memory. That's why millions of companies advertise in the yellow pages. The next time you have something you need to remember, try writing it down on a yellow post-it note or legal pad. Even children's moods can be controlled by colors. Colors affect your mood. So why wouldn't it work to help you stay calm on a flight? Well, it can!

Understanding Color Therapy

Color therapy, also known as *Chromotherapy* or *Chromatherapy,* is based on the fact that physiological functions respond to specific colors. The application of color in various ways is used for the purpose of healing and maintaining optimum health. It is a therapeutic science that has been used by many societies for thousands of years. Egyptians used specially built solarium rooms with different colored glass. The sun shone through the colored glass onto the patient to attain particular therapeutic benefits. How does this happen? Attached to the brain are pineal glands, which control your daily rhythms of life. When light enters through your eyes (or skin), it travels neurological pathways to these pineal glands. Various colors give off different wavelength frequencies and these different frequencies have different effects on physical and psychological functions. The ability to alter one's mood using colors affects all of us in some way.

During the early twentieth century, Austrian scientist and philosopher Rudolph Steiner conducted research on the therapeutic use of color. He concluded that the vibrations of colors can be reinforced by shapes and that different combinations of shape and color can produce destructive or regenerative influences on living organisms. Some schools, following Steiner's theories, have painted classrooms to correspond to the "mood" of children at various stages of development. Steiner was one of many who believe in the positive effects of color on well-being.[1]

Please keep in mind that before using complementary medical techniques you should be aware that many have not been evaluated in scientific studies. Always consult with your primary health care provider before starting any new therapeutic techniques. Colors have been effective along with medical procedures, especially on a psychological level or as preventative measures. My clients have combined the use of colors with other techniques, resulting in success and enjoyment in overcoming their fears. Once you become more acquainted with colors, you will not only have fun using them but also they will become part of your daily life, whether you are flying or not.

Colors That Affect Your Mood

AQUAMARINE: Helpful with stomach, liver and throat troubles. Effects: boosts morale, meditative, calming and peaceful.

BLACK: Associated with X-rays or disease. Effects: introverted, closed personality, depressed mood, self-confidence, power, strength, high discipline and a feeling of freedom.

BLUE: Found to be successful in the treatment of neonatal jaundice, has also been shown to be effective in the treatment of rheumatoid arthritis. Also helps asthmatics remain calmer for easier breathing. Used in reducing fevers, ulcer pain, inflammatory disorders, back problems and for the terminally ill. In one study, patients exposed to blue light for periods of up to fifteen minutes experienced a significant amount of pain relief. Blue light is used in healing scar tissue, alleviating skin and lung conditions and treating malignant and benign tumors. Scientists have also reported successful use in the treatment of psychological problems like addiction, impotence, depression and eating disorders. Effects: cooling, calming, lowers blood pressure, retards growth and decreases respiration.

GOLD: Found effective for digestive irregularity, irritable bowel syndrome, rheumatism and an underactive thyroid. Effects: helps with physical and psychological depressions, uplifting.

GREEN: The most predominant color on the planet. It balances our energy and is used to increase sensitivity and compassion. (It should never be used in cancerous or tumorous conditions or anything of a malignant nature as green stimulates cell growth.) It is believed to help heart problems. Effects: soothing, relaxing mentally as well as physically, helps those suffering from depression, relieves fatigue, soothes headaches, helps with claustrophobia, anxiety and nervousness.

GRAY: When there is a gray tint to your skin or nails, there may be congestion somewhere inside the body. Effects: light gray is tremendously soothing.

INDIGO: The strongest painkiller. Found to be effective for acute sinus problems, bronchitis, asthma, migraines, high blood pressure, overactive thyroid, diarrhea and a great antidote for insomnia. Effects: relaxes, provides a peaceful environment.

LAVENDER (a pale tint of purple): Found to be effective with anxiety, migraines and panic attacks. Effects: calming, relaxing and peaceful.

ORANGE: Found to be effective with grief, bereavement and loss. Used for treatment of asthma, bronchitis, allergies, constipation, epilepsy, mental disorders, rheumatism, torn ligaments, aching bones and intestinal cramps. Effects: energizes, stimulates appetite and digestive system.

PINK (a pale tint of red): Found to be calming in the treatment of anger management. Used in diet therapy as an appetite suppressant. Effects: relaxes muscles, tranquilizes, relieves tension and soothes. Found to be calming within minutes of exposure. It suppresses hostile, aggressive and anxious behavior. "Pink holding cells are now widely used to reduce violent and aggressive behavior among prisoners, and some sources have reported a reduction of muscle strength in inmates within 2.7 seconds. It appears that when in pink surroundings people cannot be aggressive even if they want to, because the color saps their energy."[2]

YELLOW: Found effective with color-tinted glasses for learning difficulties, muscle cramps, hypoglycemia and gallstones. The color for memory. Clears away confusion and negative thinking. Effects: energizes, relieves depression, improves memory, stimulates appetite, boosts self-esteem, can help with fears and phobias like fear of flying.

PURPLE: Found to be effective for nervousness. (It should be used sparingly. It is a "heavy" color; long exposures can be depressing.) Not a good color for children. Effects: strong relaxation to depressed mood.

RED: Found to be effective in the treatment of migraine headaches, skin problems, bladder infections, anemia and cancer. Effects: power, motivation, stimulates brain wave activity, increases blood pressure, heart rate and respiration, arouses sexuality. (Can be draining if worn for long amounts of time.)

SILVER: Found to be effective with hormones and nervousness. Effects: calming, restores equilibrium, emotional tranquilizer.

TURQUOISE: Found to be effective for the central nervous system, throat and chest. Effects: soothes emotional shock, helps you get on with your life, promotes assertiveness and goal setting.

WHITE: Full spectrum light is being used in the treatment of cancers, seasonal affective disorder (SAD), anorexia, bulimia nervosa, insomnia, jet lag, alcohol and drug dependency and to reduce overall levels of medications. Effects: calming and focusing.

Colored Foods That Affect Your Mood

BLUE/INDIGO/PURPLE foods are soothing and cooling.

- *BLUE:* Helps bring peace and relaxation (blueberries, blue potatoes)
- *INDIGO:* Helps put back structure in your life, helps heal insecurity (cabbage, potatoes, grape jelly, blueberries, gelatin, etc.)
- *PURPLE:* Helps promote leadership, heals and calms the emotionally changeable individual (plums, eggplant, purple cauliflower, sweet chocolate bell peppers, purple asparagus, acai berries, purple bananas, muscadine grapes, concord grapes, figs, purple cabbage, etc.)

GREEN foods balance the body, stimulate growth and provide a tonic for the system.

- *GREEN:* Helps improve physical stamina, heals panic, fear and apprehension (spinach, green beans, lettuce, cabbage, broccoli, asparagus, green grapes, apples, kiwi, etc.)

RED/ORANGE/YELLOW foods are stimulating, exciting and hot.

- *RED:* Helps give extra energy, helps with lethargy and tiredness (red beets, strawberries, apples, red raspberries, cherries, tomatoes, tomato soup and juice, red grapes, red peppers, etc.)
- *ORANGE:* Helps create optimism and change, heals grief and disappointment (oranges, tangerines, carrots, sweet potatoes, pumpkin squash, orange juice, apricots, pumpkins, mangoes, etc.)

- *YELLOW:* Helps encourage laughter, joy and fun, heals depression (bananas, acorn squash, yellow onions, corn, potatoes, yellow tomatoes, chickpeas, oats, pineapple, yellow apples, lemons, yellow peppers)

Antioxidant vitamins such as A, B, C, E and calcium all contribute to the benefits of these foods.

History of Colors and Healing

The therapeutic use of color in the ancient world is attributed to the Egyptian god Thoth, known to the Greeks as Hermes. Later, Hippocrates, the father of Western medicine, utilized various colored ointments and salves as remedies, as well as practicing in treatment rooms painted with shades of healing colors. In first century Rome, the physician Aurelius Cornelius Celsus wrote about the therapeutic use of color, but Christianity associated it with pagan beliefs and it was not permitted by the church. In the Middle Ages, the Arab physician Avicenna wrote about color as a symptom of disease and its use in treatment; for example: red acted as a stimulant on blood flow while yellow might reduce pain.

Even though skepticism remains regarding color therapy, modern therapists have developed the use of color in psychological testing and physical diagnosis. For example, the Lüscher color test was developed to provide a quick, detailed personality analysis based on a short color-ranking exercise.[3] You can take the Lüscher color test online at sites such as **http://www.axlife.com/luscher/**.

Psychology of Color

Each color can be psychologically correlated with your moods. Blues, purples (lavenders) and indigos are cool and calming. They will help you relax and calm your disposition. Reds (pinks), oranges and yellows are warm and friendly. They will help you feel energized, happy and joyful. If you are anxious or stressed, you could use either blues or purples, and if you are feeling sad or depressed, yellows and golds will help. Once you become familiar with the benefits and effects of colors, you will know just which colors will work for you, with whatever circumstance you're facing.

The psyche can utilize color in many ways; one way that my clients have found successful and enjoyable is "drinking your color." Due to security changes, as you are well aware, it would be difficult to bring food coloring onboard. But you can buy a bottle of water once you are through the screening process or on the plane and drop a blue candy, such as a Bottle Cap, into it and tint your water to the color or shade you need.

Alternative Medicine and Colors

Alternative medicine also uses color and light for healing. Each color vibrates at a specific frequency; colors correspond to the areas of your body with the same frequency. When you are ill, organs and glands can become out of balance, not functioning at the proper frequency. Restoring proper frequency is thought to restore health.

Holistic Approach to Color Therapy

Color therapy can be applied by "wearing the color": color therapy glasses, colored clothes, taking a color bath (tub filled with colored water), using a colored lamp or painting walls a certain color, drinking colored water, eating food of a certain color, etc.

For example, neurologists have found that children with autism may be helped by wearing colored glasses (especially red), which counteracts the over-firing of the high and mid brain. If the child is angry, orange or yellow appears to be more effective. Having the child put on a pair of these colored glasses may quickly result in a calmer, more pleasant youngster.[4]

Building Positive Energy with Colors

You will learn to build positive energy by using certain colors. With whatever energy your body or psyche may need at the time, you'll be drawn to one color more so than the others. You will be amazed to discover the impact colors can have on your psychological and overall well-being. Your color needs will usually differ from day to day or from hour to hour. Just as listening is important to communicate, you must be in tune with your feelings and take in the color that is drawing you. You have a choice to be happy and relaxed on your flight, generating your own positive energy, or you can choose to be miserable and frightened, setting up your own negative energy. What you do with what you have is what counts for making a negative situation turn around into something positive.

Color Cards

Carrying a set of color cards may help relieve anxiety. You can order color cards online; some have decorative flowers or designs. You can even find some paint store sites which provide you with color families and shades. But it is very simple and inexpensive to make your own deck of color cards.

Making Your Own Color Cards

Visit your local paint store or arts and crafts shop and pick up some large paint swatches. Cut each color swatch to the size of a playing card and glue them onto small pieces of cardboard. Choose colors from the ones listed or pick some colors of your own that attract you and make you feel relaxed or energized. Keep it simple. You want to be able to look at the card, such as an aquamarine blue, for easy breathing and calming.

NOTE: My clients also have had success using small, colored stones which can work in a similar way to provide comfort, calming and relaxation. Texture is important, such as a smooth lavender stone.

Balancing Yourself with the Color Chart

The theory behind color therapy is that as you absorb a color's energy it travels along the nervous system, moving to the part or area of the body which is in need of the energy. Your body is continuously searching for ways in which it can restore or maintain a balanced state. Your psyche will draw you to the one color most needed. I've found clients being pulled toward one or two, especially if they are from the same family (e.g., red and pink or purple and lavender). It really depends on what you need at the time.

Using a Color Chart

You may use a color chart of your choice, but I've included the one that I have used with my clients as Appendix A.

Refer to the small color samples on the back cover of this book when working with the chart. You can also explore color therapy and color charts online at **www.holisticonline.com/color/color_home.htm**, **http://www.therapycolor.com** and **www.colorquiz.com/about.html**.

1. Get comfortable in your favorite seat or area of your home, office or on the airplane.
2. Take in a deep breath, exhale and repeat.
3. Wiggle your fingers and toes, shake out your hands and relax.
4. Scan over the colors on the color chart, until your eyes focus in on one.
5. Isolate the color by pulling its card out from your color deck.
6. Soak in the color with your eyes, remembering to blink and look away occasionally.
7. Your body will need at least twenty to thirty minutes of this color energy.
8. After you feel you have spent a comfortable amount of time absorbing your color, return back to the color chart.
9. Again, scan over the colors until your eyes focus in on another color. Repeat the procedure as needed. (Usually, you'll return to the same one or two colors.)

Points to Remember

Color therapy, also known as *Chromotherapy* or *Chromatherapy*, is the application of color in various ways for the purposes of healing, maintaining balance and wellness, physically, psychologically, emotionally and spiritually. It is a therapeutic practice which has been used by many societies for thousands of years. The ability to alter your mood using color affects each and every one of us in one way or another. Color therapy is gaining popularity not only for psychological but also medical use. Even with skepticism about the use of healing with color, present-day therapists have adopted the use of color in psychological testing and physical diagnosis.

Once you become familiar with colors, their benefits and effects, you can find out which colors will work for you. You can even use colored food for your mood. Each color can be psychologically correlated with your moods. The more you familiarize yourself with which colors are cool and which are warm, their uses and the effects they will have, the more surprised you will be to see how important colors will become for you and your lifestyle. You will learn to build positive energy by using certain colors.

It will help to carry a set of color cards. They will become a way of life for you. In only a few minutes, after focusing on a specific color, you will become calm, relaxed or energized; it will give you the color energy your body and psyche needs. Perhaps color will have a new meaning for you, as you see, eat, drink or wear the color you need.

Key Questions

1. What is color therapy?
2. What colors will you use to aid relaxation?
3. How does color therapy integrate with food therapy and aromatherapy?

chapter 16

Packing and Wearing Comfortable Clothes

chapter goal:

To discuss flight attire and learn how to pack for comfortable and safe air travel so that you will be more relaxed and unencumbered.

It isn't about fashion but about safety and comfort when you fly on an airplane. Think about sitting for a long time in tight-fitting clothing; it's not fun, nor is it healthy! Also, what you wear will make a difference in the unlikely event of an emergency landing or an evacuation. Your clothing can protect your body and help to prevent physical problems – or it may contribute to them, with the wrong type of clothing. The color you select to wear can affect your level of relaxation. Also, comfortable shoes will be better for your feet, as the plane can climb and cruise for several hours and some swelling may occur.

Don't forget skincare; just like you need to hydrate with water, so does your skin. If your body is comfortable on the flight, you will be too.

Have you ever had to sit on your luggage to close it? Do you think you over-pack when you travel? Your luggage, even if pulled on wheels, can still hurt you physically. If you drive yourself to the airport, as many individuals do, you have to pick up your luggage to place it in your car and take it out when you arrive at the parking lot or garage. If you're not checking your suitcase in at the counter, which many individuals are choosing not to do, then you have to take it with you through the security checkpoint.

If you have some time before your flight (or perhaps the flight is delayed), you may decide to purchase something to eat. Remember that you can't leave your luggage alone for even a second. So pack judiciously and decide what your most important carry-on items are. There's no question: over-packing is travelers' biggest mistake.

What to Wear for Air Travel

The four concepts to keep in mind are: safety, comfort, simplicity and security.

1) **Safety**: In the unlikely event of an emergency landing or evacuation situation, you want to make sure your body is protected. There are a few simple guidelines to follow:
   - Your clothing should be made of fire-resistant material or natural fabrics such as cotton, silk, wool, leather, etc.
   - The cabin can become chilly, especially on night flights, so you want to wear clothing that will cover your arms and legs.
   - Select clothing that helps you feel safe. Use what you now know about colors; have fun!

2) **Comfort**: You want to enjoy your flight and being comfortable is important. You don't need to add extra stress.
   - Your clothing should be loosely-fitted. You can't move around as you do on the ground and sitting for hours in an airline seat can actually hurt! Realistically, tight clothing can be restricting and you don't want to be at risk for a thrombosis.
   - Layer your clothing and remember to wear pants and a long sleeve top with sleeves you can roll up if you feel warm.
   - Have a sweatshirt, sweater or light jacket on hand. The airplane doesn't maintain a constant temperature throughout the cabin and it does get cooler on night flights.
   - Bring a pair of socks to put on if your feet get cold.
   - Once again, use what you now know about colors and have fun!

3) **Simplicity**: Keep it simple! Don't choose clothing you struggle with, which can cause frustration and added stress.

- Wear layers that can be easily removed. You don't want to be hitting your neighbor with your elbow.
- If you didn't have time to change out of your business or formal attire, bring something that is light and easy to slip into. You can make the change in the lavatory.
- Place your ID in one pocket and some cash in another for easy access at the ticket counter, when going through security or after buying something at the airport. At the security checkpoint, you will have to place your items in the plastic tub to be scanned, but afterwards you don't have to bring them out again. You won't have to worry about losing your wallet or digging into your purse. I do it all the time and it makes traveling so much easier.

4) **Security**: It pays to travel safely. Don't fret over airline security rules; they've been implemented for your safety.
   - Keep your carry-on luggage with you always!
   - Be cautious and diligent at all times, whether flying or not. It's smart to be aware of your surroundings without obsessing over them.
   - Keep your money out of sight and secure.

What Not to Wear

Again, the four concepts to keep in mind are: safety, comfort, simplicity and security.

1) **Safety**:
   - Avoid synthetics, which can melt when heated, such as rayon, nylon or poly-cotton blends.
   - Avoid wearing nylon stockings while in-flight, because in the event of an evacuation down the escape slide, they can cause burns on your legs from the friction.
   - Do not wear sharp items (i.e., jagged jewelry, big belt buckles, big zippers, etc.) Also, earrings, metal hair clips and belt buckles can set off the metal detectors. The same thing goes for money clips, tie clips, cufflinks, large metal buttons and even underwire and clasps on some brassieres.

- Do not wear colors that can be aggressive, draining, depressive or represent authority and power. In the unlikely event of a terrorist attack or hijacking, colors of authority should be avoided. Use what you now know about colors; have fun!
- Do not flash your money. Keep your wallet out of sight.
- Do not expose your personal information: anything with your social security number, name, address, phone number, etc. You never know who is traveling.

2) **Comfort**:

- Don't wear clothing that exposes your arms and legs (i.e., shorts, short skirts or dresses, skimpy tops, etc.) You want to stay warm and also protect your arms and legs.
- Don't wear heavy cologne or perfume. What if you had allergies or were sensitive to scents, how would you feel if everyone on the plane wore their favorite cologne or perfume?
- Don't wear draining colors.

3) **Simplicity**:

- Don't wear layered clothes that need to go over your head or are difficult to remove.
- Don't wear anything that can slow you down. In an evacuation or emergency, you'll need to move easily and quickly.
- Don't overload your pockets with too many carry-on items.
- Don't wear excessive jewelry. It takes time at the security checkpoint and could be dangerous in an evacuation.

4) **Security**:

- Again, do not leave your carry-on items out of your sight.
- Do not obsess but stay diligent of your surroundings.
- Always observe airline policies and procedures.

It helps to know what materials and how much of them you'll need to take. In the past, traveling was somewhat different; you could check extra luggage for a minimal fee and take more than one carry-on bag. Now you need to decide what carry-on items you'll bring on your next flight.

Carry-On Items

- *Flying Fear Free:* You should be prepared for your flight, but having this book at your fingertips will allow you to look up tips and gain inspiration at any point.
- **One carry-on bag**: Travel light. You know what you really need. Make a list.
- **Medications**: Be sure medicines are in a plastic baggie for the security checkpoint. Medications, baby formula, baby food and breast milk are allowed in reasonable quantities exceeding three ounces and are not required to be in the zip-top bag. Declare these items for inspection at the checkpoint.
- **Goodie Bag and comfort box**: Add whatever you find comforting or enjoyable: color cards, magazines, pictures of your loved ones or favorite places, colored stones, music, journals, comic or joke books, coloring book and crayons, etc.
- **Snacks:** Bring any healthful food items that will relax you and keep your energy up.
- **Slippers or loose shoes:** Because your feet may swell up due to the pressurized cabin, loose slippers or shoes may be more comfortable. You should not wear tight shoes, because if you remove them in-flight it can be difficult to get them back on once the plane lands.
- **Light jacket or sweater:** You may want to put on an extra layer of clothes when the cabin temperature cools down.
- **Electronic devices or work material:** Tech gadgets like laptop computers, MP3 players, handheld devices and more are helpful in passing time.

Carry-On Items Checklist

Think through what you would like to take with you on your flight (e.g., pictures, food, favorite magazine, book, CD, etc.).

1. ______________________________

2. ______________________________

3. ______________________________

4. ______________________________

5. ______________________________

6. ______________________________

7 ______________________________

8 ______________________________

9. ______________________________

10. ______________________________

Choosing Comfortable Shoes

Leave flip-flops at home or in your luggage for when you get to your destination. You can store them in your carry-on and put them on once you get off the plane. That also goes for sandals and high-heeled shoes. In an emergency, you'll be expected to remove them before going down the evacuation slide. High heels can puncture an escape slide.

Sneakers, loosely laced tennis shoes or low-heeled slip-on shoes seem to work best for simplifying the airport security checkpoint experience. Slip-on shoes are easily removed and placed through the scanner at the checkpoint. They can also be easily removed at your seat on the airplane, if and when your feet begin to swell in-flight. You want to make it as simple and easy as possible to lower your stress level and make your flight an enjoyable experience.

If you must evacuate the airplane, sneakers and low-heeled shoes that have good traction will be more practical and safer than flip-flops or sandals, high heels, dress shoes or other shoes that have slippery soles.

Remember, at most airports, you often will have a very long hike from the gate at which you will board your flight to a connecting gate, baggage claim, customs, the parking garage to pick up your car or the exit to catch your shuttle. You will appreciate a comfortable pair of shoes, especially after a long flight.

Points to Remember

What you choose to wear is important. It isn't about fashion but about safety and comfort when you fly on an airplane. The four categories to keep in mind are safety, comfort, simplicity and security. Some important rules to keep in mind are that your clothing should be made from fire-resistant material or natural fabrics such as cotton, silk, wool or leather and be loosely fitted and layered. Have a pair of socks in case your feet get cold. Use your color therapy knowledge when selecting your clothes. Do not wear sharp objects, excessive jewelry or cologne or perfume.

Over-packing is travelers' biggest mistake. Travel light. It helps to complete a carry-on checklist and be prepared on what you should pack. Some helpful items include: this book, one carry-on bag, medications, comfort bag, snacks, slippers for in-flight, a light jacket or sweater, electronic devices and work material, etc.

More so than being fashionable, your shoes need to be comfortable! Sneakers, loosely laced tennis shoes or low heeled slip-on shoes seem to work best for simplifying the airport security checkpoint experience. Remember, your feet may swell in-flight and you will appreciate a comfortable pair of shoes, especially after a long flight!

Key Questions

1. What are the four concepts that can help you choose what to wear?
2. Why should you layer your clothes for flying on an airplane?
3. What clothes are you planning to wear for your next flight?

chapter 17

Assembling a Goodie Bag for Relaxation

chapter goals:

To address what to put in your Goodie Bag for a successful flight.

To help you in flight while keeping you from feeling silly or embarrassed and free from your fear.

As silly as it may sound, putting together items that you enjoy or that relax you will make you smile or even laugh and keep you focused on positivity. Laughter is both physically and psychologically healthy. Keep your cognitive process busy, focused and positive. A Goodie Bag can help you smile on your flight and stay relaxed.

What to Pack

Pack whatever will make you feel calm, positive and relaxed. Don't forget your healthful goodies to eat!

- **Color cards:** They can help calm or energize you, depending on what you need. Blues and purples are cool and calming. Reds and yellows are warm and energizing.
- **Box of comfort:** This is a little box filled with meaningful or comforting items (pictures, religious items, medals, charms, smooth stones, etc.)
- **Color stone:** You can lock your negative energy in a smooth color stone. Rub and feel its smoothness and let your worries transfer into and stay in the stone.

- **Pictures to visit:** Look at a picture of a loved one or a favorite place. Visit it by visualizing yourself in the picture.
- **Coloring book or colored paper and crayons:** Pick a coloring book with a theme that relaxes you. Use the color chart to pick colors that are calming.
- **Book, comic book or joke book:** Humor is healthy. Pick books that are enjoyable and comforting.
- **Relaxing music:** Pick a favorite CD or compile a relaxing playlist.

What Not to Pack

The Transportation Security Administration (TSA) website states, "The prohibited items list is not intended to be all-inclusive and is updated as necessary. To ensure travelers' security, Transportation Security Officers (TSOs) may determine that an item not on the Prohibited Items List is prohibited."[1] These items are not allowed to be carried on but may be included in your checked baggage:

- Sharp objects
- Sporting goods
- Guns and firearms
- Tools
- Martial arts and self-defense items
- Explosive and flammable materials, disabling chemicals and other dangerous items

Traveling with Alcohol

The TSA website states:

> Travelers may now carry through security checkpoints **travel-size toiletries (3 ounces or less) that fit comfortably in ONE, QUART-SIZE, clear plastic, zip-top bag**. With the exception of medications, any amount of liquid including alcohol greater than three ounces must be packed in your checked baggage. Liquids, including alcohol purchased after clearing the security checkpoint are permitted aboard aircraft.
>
> **Carrying Alcohol in Your Checked Baggage**
>
> Please note, you can't take alcoholic beverages with more than 70 percent alcohol content (140 proof), including 95

percent grain alcohol and 150 proof rum, in your checked luggage. You may take up to five liters of alcohol with alcohol content between 24 and 70 percent per person as checked luggage if it's packaged in a sealable bottle or flask.

Alcoholic beverages with less than 24 percent alcohol content are not subject to hazardous materials regulations.

Be Confident Using Your Goodie Bag

Many individuals worry about what others think, but you need to ask yourself, "Who loses if I don't take air travel?" Believe me, you may have other passengers ask to share your color cards or take part in one of your relaxation exercises. I've had clients who have had rows of passengers joining in on their fun techniques. You are your own coach, this book is your assistant coach and you may be able to coach others while on your flight. Stay positive and remember there is no room for embarrassment. You are the fortunate one; you are working on your problem and will be successfully *Flying Fear Free.*

Hazel, now a frequent flyer, always uses the techniques and exercises she learned through this program and says, "I laugh at myself and others laugh with me. From experience, I bring extra crayons and a variety of coloring books, because there are always passengers willing to join in and most are not elementary age! Now I don't have to rip out pages from my coloring book and share my box of crayons! On one flight, we experienced some turbulence and a businessman offered to pay me for my coloring book and crayons, really! So, I'll never be embarrassed when I use self-talk, draw or soak up my colors, because it's for me and who else cares? Now, if I get embarrassed, it's because I don't have enough coloring books to go around."

Bringing a Coloring Book

The type of coloring book you select and bring with you on your flight matters. You want to stay away from any theme that makes you anxious (e.g., if you don't like spiders, you don't want a coloring book with spiders, etc.). Select themes that you find enjoyable, those that put a smile on your face: the beach, nature, animals, your favorite cartoon character or a holiday theme, etc.

Refer to your color chart and review what colors you need. Stay away from colors which will cause irritation, excitement, or depressed mood (e.g., crimson or black). If you feel you need energy and you aren't far from your destination, use a pick-me-up color like green or gold.

Coloring offers several therapeutic benefits:

- It helps you take your mind off flying.
- It's another way to use color energy to relax!
- The book theme you select will also help you relax in-flight.
- During preparation for your flight, buying your special coloring book gives you motivation and keeps you positive.
- It exercises your arm and hand muscles, preventing health issues.

Building Your Box of Comfort

When preparing for your flight, make up a small box containing items that are meaningful or comforting to place in your Goodie Bag; items that evoke relaxing feelings and memories (e.g., a picture of your pet, your best friend or a beautiful garden, a note of encouragement, a poem, a prayer, a special token or medal, an aromatherapy item). Relaxing can be as easy as recalling a pleasant memory:

1. Start by taking in a deep breath of positive energy and exhale negative energy.
2. Open your box and take out one of your comfort items.
3. Use your item for comfort and feel relaxed.
4. Continue with the rest of your items or return to your box later in the flight.
5. Use self-talk: "I am enjoying myself. I feel comforted and calm."

Points to Remember

Putting together items that you enjoy or that help you relax can make you smile or even laugh, keeping you focused on the positive and not the negative. Laugher is healthy physically and psychologically. The Goodie Bag helps you bring items that will aid you in your flight. When gathering items for your Goodie Bag, pack things that will make you feel calm, happy, positive and relaxed. Add anything that comforts you and conforms to airline safety regulations.

The TSA lists the prohibited items on their website, so make sure you pack only things that will adhere to security standards.

Never feel silly when using your helpful exercises and techniques to fly fear free. Select a coloring book with a pleasant theme, bring your crayons and pick out a few magazines that interest you and pack them.

Key Questions

1. What will you pack in your Goodie Bag?
2. What can you do to curb any embarrassment you may feel about your Goodie Bag?
3. What are the benefits of a Goodie Bag?

chapter 18

Relaxing Mental Exercises for Air Travel

chapter goal:

To learn relaxing and fun psychological exercises which have been proven to help other fearful flyers and can help you to be calmer and anxiety free.

Many professionals utilize various models, techniques and theories to treat fear of flying. Some of the more successful alternative therapies include: Guided Imagery, Mental Imagery, Self-Talk, Progressive Muscle Relaxation, Breathing Exercises, Systematic Desensitization, Music Therapy, Picture Therapy, Humor Therapy, Prayer and Spirituality, and Positive Self-Coaching.

Guided Imagery

Guided Imagery is a technique that many of my clients find very helpful and enjoyable and not solely to combat the fear of flying. Guided imagery is a cognitive (thought) process which invokes and utilizes all five of your senses. You will use it to look into your mind's eye: a refreshing walk on the beach or sitting in your yard, taking in the wonderful aromas of a barbeque and the sweet, relaxing scent of your garden's soft pink roses. Guided imagery is also referred to as visualization. This technique has been used by societies over the ages as a healing tool. Guided imagery or visualization relies on dreams, fantasies, memories of your favorite events and visions to operate as a channel between your mind and body.

The ancient Greeks and Egyptians, including Hippocrates and Aristotle, believed that images discharged spirits in the brain that aroused the body and heart. The Navajo Indians practice an intricate method of imagery that inspires individuals to envision themselves as healthy. Sigmund Freud and Carl Jung both documented evidence of individuals' ability to use their imaginations to help in curing their ailments. Athletes use imagery and visualization to get in "the zone" or flow.

Modern research has found that mental images produce psychological, biochemical, physiological and immunological changes in the body that can affect physical and mental health.

Stress Management through Guided Imagery

Guided imagery/visualization has been found to be an effective tool for activating the relaxation response in individuals who are feeling stressed, anxious, overwhelmed or physically and psychologically uneasy. The nice thing about guided imagery is that it poses virtually no risk and may well provide benefits.

Guided Imagery Exercise

You may use this as one of your exercises to help you relax. But you should create a guided imagery scenario of your own, one that has meaning for you. Think of a safe place, a peaceful and enjoyable environment that you would like to see yourself in when you are feeling uneasy or unwell. You can record this in a soft, soothing tone of voice, so that you can close your eyes and relax as you listen and enter the scene. Find a place free from interruptions, loosen tight clothing, remove glasses or contacts if you'd like and get comfortable in a favorite chair, couch, bed or hammock and relax.

Guided Imagery Example: Ocean Scene

Picture and feel the sun's warm yellow rays shining down on your face and body, as a cool ocean breeze blows across your cheeks, through your hair, caressing you from your head to your toes, while you taste the salty ocean air as you gently lick your lips with delight. Take in a deep breath, let it out and relax.

Listen. You can hear the gliding, snow-white seagulls as they fly overhead through the fluffy, soft, silvery, pale pink and ivory clouds above. You can hear the aquamarine waves rolling as they come up and tickle your toes and feet. Take in a deep breath, let it out and relax. You feel safe and calm.

The sun's rays glisten over the ocean, as the waves appear to turn different shades of blue, while the clouds reflect a soft purple and pale pink across the calming, cool azure sky. A family of butterflies, with their soft velvety wings painted gold, yellow and bright orange, fly by happy and free. Take in a deep breath, let it out and relax. Let go of any anger, pain or fear.

See the warm yellow sun's glow, blanketing the golden sand so it looks as if it were dusted with sparkling diamonds, so pure, perfect and beautiful. The high tide cuddles up over your toes as you wiggle them and feel the coolness in your feet, sinking them down into the warm, comforting sand. Take in a deep breath, let out negative thoughts, pain or fear as you exhale, blowing them far away as you feel safe, content and relaxed.

As you walk along the soothing, tranquil beach, take in a deep breath of the fresh blue ocean's clean air, as you smell the sweet scent of calming lavender. Listening more deeply, you hear birds' wings beating overhead, as the birds sing out with cheerful, chirping calls that sound like a choir of angels. Take in another deep breath of the refreshing ocean air, as a gentle breeze blows its soft wind across your face and over your warm and relaxed body. You feel peaceful, rested, positive, strong, energized, healthy, happy and safe.

My Guided Imagery:

____

____

____

____

____

____

____

____

____

____

____

____

____

____

____

____

____

____

____

____

____

____

____

____

____

____

____

Exploring Progressive Muscle Relaxation (PMR)

A popular and effective technique developed by Edmund Jacobson, a physiologist formerly at the Laboratory for Clinical Physiology in Chicago, is *Progressive Muscle Relaxation (PMR)*, where a series of stress-reducing exercises is practiced. Passengers find this technique helpful, especially during turbulence.

The American Psychological Association informed readers in *Monitor on Psychology* of the important acute and long-term effects that psychological support, cognitive-behavioral therapy and an eclectic approach can have on the psyche.

Practicing PMR

You should practice this procedure and get comfortable with it. The more you use it, the more familiar your body will be with it. When you are stressed, your muscles naturally tighten up, so you are going to self-induce this feeling and teach your body what it needs to do when you and your muscles stress. Initially, it will take you three to five tries until your body learns what to do. After your body becomes introduced to this technique, it will soon know what it must do. I have had clients and patients who fall asleep before getting through the exercise, on the first run. It is a great technique to use while flying on the plane and very helpful for insomnia, too. You can record this in your soft, soothing voice, so that you can close your eyes as your body learns to relax. Always, find a place free from interruptions, loosen tight clothing, remove glasses or contacts if you'd like and get comfortable in a favorite chair, couch, bed or hammock, relax, take in a deep breath and exhale.

PMR Exercise

Starting with your feet and working up through your body to your head and neck, tense each muscle group for at least five seconds and then relax the muscles for up to thirty seconds. Before moving on to the next muscle group, repeat three to five times (it will be less as your body conditions and becomes familiar with learning how to relax). The recommendation is that you practice progressive muscle relaxation at least once or twice each day to get the maximum benefit. Each session should last approximately ten minutes.

TOES: Curl under your toes and hold; count slowly (*one thousand one, one thousand two...*) to five. Relax. Repeat three to five times.

FEET: Flex your feet toward you and hold; count to five. Relax. Repeat three to five times. Point your feet away from you, like a ballerina, and hold; count to five. Relax. Repeat three to five times.

LOWER LEG: Tighten your lower leg muscles (anterior, lateral and posterior compartments) and hold; count to five. Relax. Repeat three to five times.

UPPER LEG: Tighten your thigh/upper leg muscles and hold; count to five. Relax. Repeat three to five times.

GLUTEALS: Tighten your hips and buttocks by squeezing in and hold; count to five.

ABDOMEN: Tighten your abdomen by squeezing in your stomach and hold; count to five. Relax. Repeat three to five times.

BACK: Sit up tall and push your back forward and hold; count to five. Relax. Repeat three to five times.

CHEST: Tighten your chest by curling your shoulders in and hold; count to five. Relax. Repeat three to five times.

ARMS: Make a fist in both hands, bend your arms and squeeze them tightly up against the sides of your body and hold; count to five. Relax. Repeat three to five times.

SHOULDERS: Lift your shoulders up toward your ears and hold; count to five. Relax. Repeat three to five times.

NECK: Tilt your head to the left and hold; count to five. Relax. Repeat three to five times. Tilt your head to the right and hold; count to five. Relax. Repeat three to five times.

HEAD/FACE: Scrunch your face up like a raisin and hold; count to five. Relax. Repeat three to five times.

Practice progressive muscle relaxation at least once or twice each day to get the maximum benefit.

My Progressive Muscle Relaxation Progress:

____

____

____

____

____

____

____

____

____

Many of my clients use PMR as a part of their daily activities. PMR helps me relax and fall asleep quickly, especially after a stressful day! Many of my colleagues have reported client success with the use of PMR.

Benefits of Self-Talk

Self-talk is just that: a conversation that takes place in your mind, between you and yourself. We all do it! For example: when you see a delicious piece of cake, you might say (in your mind), "Wow, does that look heavenly!" or when you do something pretty terrific, like hit a homerun with the bases loaded, you might say (in your mind), "I did it!" or before taking an exam or giving a presentation, you might say (in your mind), "I can do this, no sweat!"

There are two types of self-talk, positive and negative:

1). **Positive (PST)**: Builds self-esteem, supports, motivates to reach goals, open to accomplish and overcome obstacles, ready to take on challenges, willing to try and usually successful.

2). **Negative (NST)**: Lowers self-esteem, is unsupportive, does not motivate to reach a goal, closed to accomplishing and overcoming obstacles, reluctant to take on challenges, unwilling to try and usually unsuccessful.

Initiate positive self-talk to bring positive things to mind; you can feel better about yourself, make better decisions and present well. Say goodbye to negative self-talk when it comes to your mind; you may not feel so sure about yourself, perhaps not make the best decisions and not present as well as you could under stress.

Some may feel that staying positive when facing a frightening situation, such as the fear of flying, can set one up for failure. Staying positive will help you to stay focused; use what you have learned and be more confident.

Exploring Breathing Exercises

How do you breathe when you're frightened or stressed? Have you ever watched someone else who was afraid? When people get frightened, stressed or anxious, they usually exhibit rapid, shallow breathing. This type of breathing contributes to and is associated with other symptoms of these triggers such as tachycardia (rapid heart rate), dry mouth and perspiration. *Diaphragmatic breathing* (relaxed breathing) can help you control your breathing before the symptoms spiral out of your control.

Breathing Exercises

1. **Relax.** Get comfortable; gently place both your hands over your abdomen.
2. **Inhale.** Keeping your mouth closed and your shoulders relaxed, with both feet resting on the ground, inhale slowly and as deeply as you possibly can while counting silently to five. While you breath in, your hands will feel your abdomen expand, allowing the air to fill your diaphragm.
3. **Hold.** Slowly count silently to three while holding the air in your lungs.
4. **Exhale.** Slowly count silently to five as you exhale the air through your mouth.
5. **Repeat.** Three to five times.

My Breathing Exercise Progress:

____

____

____

____

____

____

____

Music Therapy

Music has been used throughout history in healing rituals. In the 1950s it was recognized as a professional therapy; musicians were asked to help treat military personnel in the United States and different creative arts were used in the treatment of psychiatric disorders. Music has been found to be helpful in an individual's treatment, both physically and psychologically. Therapists have used music by having individuals listen to a song and then discuss the piece of music, in order to help the patient express his or her feelings. Music is also used as a relaxation technique. Music therapists are professionals, trained and certified, working in hospitals, clinics, drug and alcohol treatment programs, prisons, long-term care facilities and hospices.

Throughout my years of experience in the medical and psychological fields and as a practicing musician, I have found music to be an important part of the healing process and effective for relaxation (e.g., illness, driving, studying, dental work, pregnancy and delivery, anger management, insomnia, phobias, etc.). It is easy to use, has negligible side effects and you can choose the music that best fits your need: relaxation, motivation, energy, uplifting, spiritual, etc.

Studies have found that music therapy reduces blood pressure, heart rate, anxiety and tension. It has also been found successful in reducing aggressiveness, improving mood and willingness in Alzheimer's patients. It helps individuals with autism to learn communication skills, can increase the effectiveness of some antidepressant medications and can improve mood in individuals with job burnout and those undergoing cancer treatment.

Using music with a guided imagery exercise or progressive muscle relaxation can be very effective. Several of my clients relax with a combination of these exercises after a stressful day at work, a difficult situation in their personal lives, before taking an exam or taking a flight. It is also helpful to select music that is relaxing to you. Songs with a sixty-beat-per-minute rhythm are most helpful. This tempo matches the resting heart rate and will help you slow down and rest, especially for insomnia. Choose and relax with the kind of music you like.

Art Therapy

If you have difficulty talking about your fear of flying, it may be helpful to draw, paint or sculpt to let out your expressions and organize your thoughts and emotions. It is therapeutic to bring out your inner thoughts and feelings with an art creation, and to take the time for interpretation of your artwork. Much can be told from a piece of art. Be creative and bring out the tension and anxiety that has built up within you.

Picture Therapy

Placing yourself in a picture can be very therapeutic. Select a few of your favorite pictures and immerse yourself in them. Whenever you are feeling uneasy or anxious, it can help to look at your pet puppy, your flower garden or your favorite golf course and do some imagery; feel your fuzzy little friend licking your face or smell the fragrance of your beautiful flowers or take that swing on the twelfth fairway. Take time and select a few calming and fun pictures to pack in your Goodie Bag for your flight.

Humor Therapy

You can use cognitive therapy and revise the way you think with humor. You can start looking for humor in your situation and use it to stop your worries. Studies have found that laughter can lower your blood pressure, help with depression, defuse anger and get you through a stressful situation like flying.

Laughter is not only an effective stress-reliever, but it also can be heart healthy. One study presented at the American College of Sports Medicine researched the harmful cardiovascular toll of stress and negative mood:[1]

"A small group of healthy adults were instructed to watch either a comedy or documentary film, and were monitored for carotid artery activity during the films. Subjects who watched the comedy benefited from improved 'arterial compliance,' the amount of blood that moves through the arteries at a given time. Conversely, decreased arterial compliance is often associated with high blood pressure and heart disease."

Read a comic book or joke book or listen to a comedy album while onboard to help relieve stress.

Writing Therapy

Writing is a great way to express your feelings and emotions; there is no right or wrong, you are just talking to the paper. Use a sheet of pastel paper or buy a special book to journal in so that you can have it as a keepsake and, for future flights, learn from your experiences.

Don't be afraid to write about the anxiety you may feel at a given moment. You may be surprised at what you put on the page! Seeing your thoughts in words helps you to contextualize and handle any fear and anxiety.

Mental Imagery

Elite athletes talk a lot about being in "the zone," that magical place where the mind and body work in perfect synch and their movements flow without conscious effort.

Former pro hockey player Wayne Gretzky and golfer Tiger Woods are exemplary users of imagery and visualization, with focus and concentration skills superior to other players.

You can "stay in the zone" by working on your fear, practicing the techniques and exercises, "listening" to your body and "reading" your muscles to work to calm it all down by bridging your mind and body.

Visualize Yourself Handling Fear

Always find a place free from interruptions, loosen tight clothing, remove glasses or contacts if you'd like and get comfortable in a favorite chair, couch, bed or hammock; relax, take in a deep breath, exhale, another deep breath in, exhale, letting out any uneasy feelings and breathe in calmness, energy and confidence. Feel yourself whole, in control and balanced and use positive self-talk: "I can do this!" "I can and I will!"

Visualize the sun shining its golden rays down on you and the warmth penetrating down through your head and body as it heals you, gives you energy, a feeling of peace and power, with a calming effect that makes you feel relaxed and safe. As the warm golden light passes through to your toes, it takes with it all your built-up negative energy, any pain you have, as well as your fear of flying, and sends it out through your toes and far away from you. You feel powerful. Acknowledge any leftover feelings of fear. Recall your list of what you are fearful of. Take each fear and tell it that there is no room for it in your mind or body and send it with the light, as it leaves your body through your toes and travels far away. Realize that as the fear flows in and flows right back out, there is no room in your mind or body for it and you must tell it so any time you feel it sneak in. Begin to voice affirmations about your fears: "I am strong and powerful. I have courage. I trust myself and know that I can do this. I can and I will!"

Visualize yourself handling the situation you fear in a comfortable, calm, relaxed and powerful manner. You are handling your anxiety, worries and stress. You are feeling strong and in control. You know that you are worthy to fly without fear. Acknowledge your fear and watch it leave, let it go. Slowly let your negative images and feelings fade, drift away, remembering that you can do whatever you wish to do. You can fly successfully, without fear; you deserve to and you've earned the right to enjoy your flight!

On the count of three, open your eyes, feeling relaxed, powerful, courageous and confident.

Meditation

Many people use meditation for relaxation, health and well-being. The term refers to a group of techniques, most with roots in Eastern spiritual traditions.

When you meditate, you focus on your breathing or repeating a word, sound, chant or phrase, shelving thoughts which ordinarily inhabit your conscious mind. Meditating is believed to take you to a state of physical relaxation, mental serenity, attentiveness and psychological balance. Meditation can help you to control how you react to a difficult or challenging situation. It can change how you respond to the flow of emotions and cognitive processes (thoughts). Once you learn how to meditate, you can do it on your own. It can also be practiced as a part of another mind-body therapy (e.g., tai chi).

Meditation has been found to treat a variety of problems such as pain, depression, stress, anxiety, insomnia, grief, fear, asthma, fibromyalgia and high blood pressure.

Spirituality and Prayer

Spirituality has many definitions; it isn't essentially connected to a particular belief group or religion. It has to do with your connection with yourself and with others, your search for meaning and your personal values. Most associate spirituality with prayer, religion, meditation or a belief in a higher power. For some, it can be found in music, art, nature, objects or a secular community. Spirituality has its own meaning for each individual.

Spirituality starts with the relationship you have with yourself. It is nurtured by the relationships you have with others and ends in a feeling of your purpose in life. There are ways you can foster your spirituality, enrich your self-esteem, further your relationships with others who are important to you, appreciate yourself and who you are.

Many individuals use spirituality by praying for themselves, for their situations and for others. Many churches have prayer groups for sick members of their community. Although scientific research is in the early stages of determining the effectiveness of prayer on physical and mental health, there is reason to believe that prayer and religious observance are associated with better mental and physical health and a longer, happier, more fulfilled life.

In the past and still today, many counselors and therapists remain hesitant to touch on clients' faiths, beliefs and religious identities as part of the therapeutic process. Times are changing and many professionals are moving forward to incorporate spirituality and religion in their clients' treatment plans.

A lot of people use prayer in stressful situations, such as before an exam, a surgical procedure or a frightening situation like flying, and it is their faith in a higher power that helps get them through. Many clients I work with pray to deities, saints or figures in their religion who make them feel safe.

Positive Self-Coaching

You are your own coach and this book is your assistant coach. You will not only be your own coach but also your cheerleader! You know the game plan, you practiced the plays and you're getting better and better at your game, flying without fear in an airplane. As you practice the exercises and techniques, you will experience "flow," extreme well-being during the activity. Go back and read your self-talk and start using it, coach. Positive self-coaching can be supportive and rewarding!

Systematic Desensitization

You have learned to associate your feelings of anxiety, discomfort, nervousness and avoidance with your fear of flying. You will learn a new set of feelings associated with air travel, such as relaxation, comfort, calmness and enjoyment.

The purpose of systematic desensitization is to teach you to relax with your trigger (e.g., fear of flying), imagining various steps related to your fear of flying while you are relaxed. It is based on counter-conditioning, as you learn a new conditioned response (relaxation) that is incompatible with or inhibits the old conditioned response (fear and anxiety). Most individuals avoid thinking about their fear, because it is uncomfortable and usually makes them anxious. The goal is that after using systematic desensitization, you will be able to think about your trigger (flying) and imagine it clearly in detail and not feel anxious, but instead relaxed. After daily, repeated practice, you will decrease your anxiety not only while imagining a flight, but also, most importantly, in the real world. You will become a comfortable and confident flyer.

Begin the desensitization process with the least frightening step, such as packing for your flight, versus takeoff or landing.

Three Systematic Desensitization Steps

1) **Relaxation Training:** Use relaxation techniques or exercises to relax yourself. Combine a relaxation exercise with the situation (e.g., progressive muscle relaxation).
2) **Anxiety Hierarchy:** The hierarchy is a list of situations involving your trigger behavior (e.g., flying) that cause your anxiety.
   - Think through and write down the situations involving your fear of flying. Now arrange your list of situations from least uncomfortable to most uncomfortable, as you imagine yourself there in that situation.

     Note: The usual number of hierarchy situations is anywhere from ten to twenty items.
   - After creating your hierarchy, write out each item on a separate index card and number each card in its proper order.
3) **Systematic Desensitization Sessions:** You will practice repetitive systematic desensitization sessions regularly, every day.
   - To begin each session, you will use your relaxation technique to become relaxed.
   - Next, you will imagine the first situation on your anxiety hierarchy while in a relaxed state. You must repeatedly imagine the step until you are free of anxiety when imaging it.
   - Once you are comfortable with the present situation, you will progress to the next higher anxiety-producing situation on your hierarchy, until you reach the highest, most frightening step.
   - The anxiety will gradually decrease with each hierarchy step, until you can reach your last step, your flight without fear!

Relax! Prior to beginning your systematic desensitization session, spend thirty minutes each day practicing your relaxation exercises and techniques. Once you feel ready to begin, for relaxation to be effective please observe these guidelines:

Guidelines for Effective Relaxation

1. Practice for at least thirty minutes, every other day or more, while relaxing and imagining each step of your hierarchy.
2. Do your sessions in the same relaxing setting each time.
3. Conduct your relaxation and systematic desensitization sessions in a darkened and quiet room. Be comfortable throughout the sessions. Choose your favorite chair, couch, bed, hammock, etc.
4. Be sure your relaxing and systematic desensitization sessions are uninterrupted.
5. Practice the relaxation techniques as instructed.
6. It can help to practice your relaxation exercises at other times also. This aids your body to become familiar with relaxing. It's a great way to fall asleep at night!
7. You'll be ready to start your systematic desensitization session when you can relax completely in three to five minutes as you briefly practice your relaxation exercises.
8. Imagine the items in the situation vividly (e.g., the sounds, sights, textures, tastes, colors and smells). If you cannot completely relax in three to five minutes while vividly imagining the items, you are not ready. Keep working on this step until you are 100 percent relaxed. You should feel as relaxed as you do when you practice your relaxation exercises without thinking of the situation.
9. When you feel anxious imagining the situation, stop and return to your relaxation exercises or imagine a peaceful scene. After you are once again relaxed, you may return to your hierarchy and move on to the next step.
10. If you are experiencing problems with continual anxiety in a step, you may need to rearrange your hierarchy or add some additional less stressful situations before moving on to the problem step. You may not be ready for this step; you need to build upward through your hierarchy, while using your relaxation exercises.

Check the order of your index cards regarding your anxiety level. The goal is to try and get an order that works for you, presenting an even progression of anxiety from low to high. The goal is to feel absolutely relaxed through each situation.

Hierarchy of Fearful Steps

This exercise gives you an example, so you can create your own "Hierarchy of Steps":

1. Making flight reservations
2. Packing luggage
3. Driving to the airport
4. Finding a parking space
5. Taking the escalator to the ticket counter area
6. Going to the ticket counter and checking your luggage
7. The reality of having to fly
8. Sitting at the gate and waiting to board the plane
9. Hearing the boarding announcement
10. Plane doors closing and announcements made for departure
11. Plane taxiing
12. In-flight service
13. Going to the lavatory
14. Moving around the cabin
15. Climbing to cruising altitude
16. Looking out the window
17. Takeoff
18. Descending
19. Landing
20. Turbulence

My Hierarchy of Steps for Fear of Flying

Arrange your list of situations from the least uncomfortable to the most uncomfortable as you imagine yourself there in that situation. Relax.

1. ______________________________
2. ______________________________
3. ______________________________
4. ______________________________
5. ______________________________
6. ______________________________
7. ______________________________
8. ______________________________
9. ______________________________
10. ______________________________
11. ______________________________
12. ______________________________
13. ______________________________
14. ______________________________
15. ______________________________
16. ______________________________
17. ______________________________
18. ______________________________
19. ______________________________
20. ______________________________

Points to Remember

Many professionals utilize various models, theories and techniques in treating fear of flying. Some alternatives include Guided Imagery, Mental Imagery/Visualization or "Staying in the Zone,"

Progressive Muscle Relaxation, Self-Talk, Systematic Desensitization, Music Therapy, Picture Therapy, Humor Therapy, Breathing Exercises, Prayer and Spirituality, Positive Self-Coaching, etc.

Practice the techniques you learned in this chapter to be successful.

Key Questions

1. What therapeutic steps are you inclined to try?
2. How can these techniques be applied to other parts of your life?
3. What technique do you anticipate will be the most successful in overcoming your fear of flying?

chapter 19

Relaxing Physical Exercises for Air Travel

chapter goal:

To explain helpful physical exercises that can be performed in-flight that aid physical and mental relaxation.

Whether traveling by road, rail or airplane, muscles can become tight and achy. In an airplane, you will be in your seat with your seat belt fastened for the majority of the flight. This chapter gives you exercises to use while taking air travel that will help relax your muscles, especially when you are feeling tense or stressed.

The Gymnast

Any kind of travel, especially air travel, can cause stiffness and achiness in your muscles. This is especially true in your legs, which can succumb to mild yet uncontrollable shaking or twitching. You can help prevent this by conditioning your legs while in-flight and sitting in your seat by practicing the *Gymnast*. Like a football player preparing for a game or an Olympic gymnast before an event, it helps to stretch out your muscles. It's easy to employ the Gymnast:

1. Start by stretching your feet forward under the seat in front of you.
2. Slightly lift one foot off the floor, pointing your toes toward the cockpit; hold and count to five.

3. Flex your foot upward so your toes are pointing toward the ceiling of the cabin; hold and count to five.
4. Relaxing both feet on the floor of the plane, take in a deep breath, exhale and self-talk, "I feel relaxed. I can and I will!"
5. Repeat exercise with your other foot.
6. Repeat exercise three to five times with each foot until relaxed.

When the seat belt sign is not illuminated, you can walk in the aisle to stretch out your legs, while feeling more in control of the situation.

The Funny Face

Tension can cause tightness in your jaw and neck. Your temporomandibular joint (TMJ) can become tense and painful and it may even require medication to loosen the jaw. Making the *Funny Face* can help you relax it with humor:

1. Start by puffing up your cheeks with air and slowly releasing the air through your lips like a deflating balloon, until you have "fish lips." Now nicker (blow air out through your lips like a horse) five times. Relax.
2. From "fish lips" you will now pretend that you are an ape, extending your lower jaw forward as far as you can, trying to extend it past your teeth in the upper jaw. Hold and count to five.
3. Relax your jaw by bringing it back and gently dropping it open. Hold and count to five, then gently close with self-talk, "I feel relaxed and tension is leaving."
4. Repeat exercise three to five times until relaxed.

The Sea Turtle

Any stress or tension can cause tightness in your neck and shoulders. It is easy to relax these muscles by using the *Sea Turtle*:

1. Start by sitting straight in your seat with your seat belt fastened.
2. Trying to make your neck disappear like a sea turtle, simultaneously shrug your shoulders and try to touch the tips of your ears with the tops of your shoulders. Hold and count to five.

3. Relax your shoulders by dropping them and then rotating them forward and back twice to release the tension.
4. Repeat exercise three to five times until relaxed.

Step Relaxation

A very simple imagery exercise, *step relaxation,* will help you feel calmer as you relax with each step, slowly counting backwards from seven to one, exhaling on each step:

1. Start by imagining yourself standing at the top of a flight of seven steps.
2. Take in a deep breath and exhale while descending down from the seventh step.
3. As you descend down to the next step, you will become more relaxed.
4. Repeat each procedure for each step as you get closer to complete relaxation.
5. When you reach the bottom step, you will feel completely calm.
6. Use self-talk, "I am calm, relaxed and just fine!"
7. Repeat exercise if you are not totally relaxed.

Tension Points

If you feel tense in certain parts of your body, a *tension points* exercise will help you let go of the built-up stress. You will check your stressful body parts by pressing different muscles in places such as your temple, neck, jaw, shoulders and so on, to see if you are storing built-up tension. Then you will use these steps to relax those areas:

1. Start with one of your stressed body parts (e.g., neck). You can first generate natural body heat by rubbing your hands together and then placing them over the tense area or pressing in lightly and give yourself a gentle mini-massage. (It helps to close your eyes.)
2. Mentally, tell yourself to relax and visualize the body part letting go of tension.
3. Take a slow, deep breath in of positive energy and exhale negative energy.

4. Repeat for each body tension point.
5. Self-talk, "I am relaxed."
6. Repeat until you feel the tension totally gone.

Foot Massage

This exercise is derived from the practice of *reflexology,* which is based on the principle that various spots in your feet and hands correspond to different parts of the body; you massage your feet to improve circulation and relieve tension in specific body parts or organs. With the consideration of air travel, we will focus on the upper and middle back, which can feel tense while sitting for hours in an airline seat:

1. Start by applying pressure to the arch of your foot, because that spot corresponds to your spinal vertebrae.
2. Repeat exercise with your other foot.
3. Take in a deep breath, exhale and relax.

Give Yourself a Micro-Massage

Little massages can feel good. If you are traveling with someone, it can be not only relaxing to share a *micro-massage,* but fun too!

1. Start by taking in a slow deep breath and let it out.
2. Give attention to the smaller parts of your body (e.g., eyebrows, face, ears, scalp, hands, arms, knees, ankles and feet).
3. Self-talk, "This feels great! I am relaxed."

Hydrate Your Face and Skin

The airplane cabin is very dry and just as you can become dehydrated, so can your face. Hydrate and splash your face during air travel. Find a moisturizing facial mist whose scent and feel you enjoy. But you must follow security regulations; at the security checkpoint, you will only be allowed to carry a bottle that holds 3.4 ounces (100ml) or less (by volume).

Bring three rose petals, preferably pink, placed in a one-quart-size, clear plastic zip-top bag along with a small 3.4 ounce spray bottle. Buy a bottle of water once you get past the security checkpoint or on the plane. Fill your spray bottle with water and add your rose petals. You are ready to give your face a splash of energy! A simple spray bottle filled with water and rose petals can be a quenching drink for your face:

1. Start out by taking a walk to the lavatory with your spray bottle.
2. Close your eyes, then generously spray a refreshing and energizing mist all over your face.
3. Repeat throughout your flight as needed. Recommendation: one mist drink per hour of flight.
4. Relax while feeling refreshed!

Points to Remember

This chapter gives you several quick, easy, effective exercises to use while flying (or anytime!) that will help relax your muscles or energize you, especially when you are feeling tense or stressed, exhausted from your long day or your flight. It is helpful to have exercises at your fingertips that are quick and easy. Try fun and relaxing exercises like the *Gymnast*, the *Funny Face* and the *Sea Turtle*; use meditation or give yourself a massage.

Key Questions

1. Which techniques can you practice while at home?
2. Which technique do you most look forward to doing on your next flight?
3. How do you think physical relaxation aids mental relaxation?

chapter 20

Developing Your Flight Plan

chapter goals:

To address how to prepare for the flight using a thought stopping process and discuss other easy techniques to do before and during your flight.

To teach you how to develop your own flight plan.

The key to a successful flight is to lower your stress. To do that, it helps to create your own flight plan. It will assist you with visualizing and practicing your itinerary. It helps to have something to use for immediate relief of your fear, such as a *thought stopping process* which can help you stop your fearful thoughts promptly. You will want to measure your fear so that you can have a way to monitor and assess your improvement and discover which exercises and techniques work best for your fear. You should know what to do before your flight, such as taking practice runs to the airport to familiarize yourself with the flight procedure prior to your flight date. It can be helpful to meet the flight crew and inform them that you are a fearful flyer. Simulating your flight with guided imagery is a great way to lower your stress and fear.

Stop Racing Thoughts

When your thoughts start careening out of control, you need to put on the brakes! You can do so through a technique called *thought stopping,* a process that is easy, quick and very effective. It can be used in addiction treatment: as the thought of alcohol or drugs enters one's mind, one self-talks, "Stop!" and redirects the thought and urge. There are some professionals who argue that it's not effective to suppress the thoughts, and they return later causing a problem for the individual. This is why an eclectic approach to the fear of flying is so important. The thought stopping process works immediately when you need something to interrupt your negative thoughts and emotions, but you should use the wealth of information that you have learned once you are back in your positive train of thought. You need a multi-therapeutic approach. The principles of why thought stopping works are rather straightforward. Interrupting worrisome and needless thoughts with a "Stop!" command acts as a reminder and a distraction. Phobic thoughts are inclined to repeat in your mind. When unchecked, they become automatic and strike repeatedly. When using the thought stopping process, you become aware of unhealthy thought strings, while diverting your attention from destructive, negative, recurring cognitive routines. Using the thought stopping technique can give you a feeling of control and power. When followed with positive and reassuring self-talk, it breaks the negative thought cycle and replaces it with positivity and encouragement.

Five Thought Stopping Steps:

1. *Identify* the negative thought and decide you will not welcome it!
2. Take a*ction* by visualizing a STOP sign and snap the palm of your hand with a rubber band that you place around your hand prior to leaving home (can be a calming color).
3. Employ *self-talk* by telling yourself to stop thinking the negative thought.
4. *Replace* the negative thought by reminding yourself with a positive thought or image that "I am in control!" "I can and I will!"
5. *Continue* the process by repeating steps one through four as often as you need.

Measuring Fear with SUDS

Measure your fear of flying, so you can set your goals about what you need to do for your flight plan. My clients have found Joseph Wolpe's Subjective Units of Disturbance Scale (SUDS) helpful.[1] This is a *subjective scale*; you measure your own fear.

#100) Think about when you've been totally frightened or scared; when you're at your maximum fear level (as frightened or scared as you can get). You may have not experienced being on a plane yet, but you may imagine the fear as many fearful flyers often do when they don't know what to expect.
#50) Think about being somewhere in the middle between being totally relaxed and totally frightened.
#1) Think about when you're absolutely relaxed (at the beach or comfy under blankets as you fall asleep).

Now you need to learn to measure your fear by recalling your last flight. On a scale of 1 to 100, how frightened were you during each step of the flight? What was your SUDS score when you made your reservation? While packing your luggage? When you were going to the airport? At the ticket counter? Enter your score in the table for each of these stages of your flight process. Continue to use the SUDS scores to measure your fear and progress.

You can also use your SUDS scores to decide if these exercises and techniques are working. If they are, you may lower your SUDS score while you are actually in-flight. As your scores get lower, you will start to accept the fact that you are in control of your fear. Use this to set goals for yourself, too.

My SUDS Scores

		Reservations	Going to Airport	At the Gate	Takeoff	Cruise	Descent	Landing
Totally Frightened	100							
Moderately Frightened	50							
Totally Relaxed	1							

Set Goals Using SUDS

After using SUDS to measure your fear, list your goals. Use your exercises and techniques, such as systematic desensitization, to work through each part. Also, this is where you can use your thought stopping process.

Setting My Goals Example

Phases of your flight	SUDS Score
Making reservations	10
Takeoff	50
Descending	50
Landing	100

Other Problems: I feel sick to my stomach when I see a plane in the sky.

Setting My Goals

Phases of your flight	SUDS Score

Other Problems: ____________________

Flight Plan Example

This example will help you make your own flight plan. List your fears and the exercises and techniques which you find helpful in eliminating those fears. Take your time to develop your flight plan.

Waiting at the Departure Gate

1. Don't sit near the windows.
2. If looking out a window at the plane, don't focus down at the ground.

Boarding the Plane

1. Board last so I don't have to wait on the jet bridge by the door of the plane.

2. Stay focused on looking down the aisle, locating my seat and not looking out the windows.
3. Make sure to find the aisle or middle seat that I requested/selected on reservation.
4. If no one is sitting in the window seat, pull down the shade after the plane is airborne.
5. Avoid looking out the window and down at the ground.

What to Do with Fear

1. Use color cards, guided imagery, progressive muscle relaxation.
2. Put on colored glasses.

How to Eliminate Panic

1. Use thought stopping process:
   a. Identify negative thoughts.
   b. Take action (visualize STOP sign and SNAP rubber band).
   c. Self-Talk, "STOP."
   d. Replace/Remind, "I can and I will!"
   e. Continue if needed.
2. Control breathing with hands resting on abdomen.
3. Listen to music.
4. Smell lavender spray on wrist.

Pre-Flight Checklist

Before your flight date, make several practice runs to the airport to familiarize yourself with what to expect.

- Time yourself on how long it takes to get to the airport (notice if there is road construction, etc.).
- Once at the airport, find long or short-term parking. Park your car, making note of the parking fee.
- Make yourself comfortable with sights, sounds and smells using your techniques and exercises as needed (thought stopping as you hear and see planes taking off and landing, etc.).
- Find your airline's ticket counter and watch while acquainting yourself with the procedure, seeing if there is a kiosk available.
- Find the security checkpoint and observe the procedures; you will not be permitted past this point.

- Spend some time in the terminal familiarizing yourself with the environment; get lunch or dinner or grab a snack or beverage.

Flight Simulation with Guided Imagery

This will help you prepare for a successful flight. Take your time using visualization.

1. The night before, pack just what is needed (travel light and follow airline security rules).
2. Pack your Goodie Bag.
3. Get to bed early (set alarm with at least thirty minutes to spare).
4. Eat a light meal before leaving for the airport (no caffeine, alcohol, sugar, salt, fatty or gassy foods).
5. Leave the house with plenty of time to get to the airport.
6. Travel to the airport.
7. Park.
8. Enter the terminal.
9. Check in at the ticket counter or use electronic ticketing.
10. Pass through security.
11. Arrive at your departure gate.
12. Board the plane.
13. Push back from the gate.
14. Taxi from the gate to the runway.
15. Take off.
16. Cruise.
17. Experience turbulence.
18. Descend toward your destination.
19. Land.

What to Do When You Board the Plane

1. If you are feeling uncomfortable before boarding your plane, use a guided imagery exercise while waiting.
2. Control your breathing with a deep breathing exercise:
   a. **Inhale:** count silently to five.
   b. **Hold:** count silently to three.

c. **Exhale:** Slowly count silently to five, exhaling the air through your mouth.

3. Once onboard, you may want to meet the crew and it doesn't hurt to let them know you are an uncomfortable flyer.
4. Locate your seat, counting the rows to the closest exit; place your luggage in the overhead compartment or underneath the seat in front of you. Get comfortable in your seat.
5. Open the air vent directly above your seat (on the cabin ceiling) on your Customer Service Unit. Remember, many airlines have decided to omit them on newer wide-bodies.
6. Ask the flight attendant for a blanket and pillow if you plan on sleeping.
7. Make sure your seat is in its upright position and the tray table in front of you is closed and secured.
8. Make sure all your carry-on items are stowed, such as a briefcase, purse, etc.
9. Fasten your seat belt low and comfortably tight.
10. Open your magazine, visit a picture, use your color cards or any other exercise or technique which you find helpful.
11. Listen to the PA and watch the flight attendant or video demonstration while following along with the safety information card, usually found in the seat pocket in front of you. Follow all instructions.
12. Relax. Use your exercises and techniques as needed. You're ready for takeoff!

Points to Remember

To lower your stress, creating your own flight plan can help you calm down. It helps to have something to use for immediate relief of your fear, such as a thought stopping process which can assist you to stop your fearful thoughts rapidly! You will want to measure your fear so you can assess your progress and determine which exercises and techniques work best for your fear, using SUDS. You will set your goals from your discovery. Utilize your exercises and techniques, such as *systematic desensitization,* to work through each part. Simulating the flight with guided imagery will prepare you for a successful flight. In your flight plan, list your discovered fears and the exercises and techniques which you find helpful. Use a guided imagery exercise while waiting to board if you are feeling uneasy. It will be helpful to know what to do when you board the plane. Before your date of departure, it's a good idea for you to make practice runs to the airport to familiarize yourself with the flight procedure and environment.

Key Questions

1. Can you list the five thought stopping steps?
2. What will you use to measure your fear?
3. How does taking practice trips to the airport prior to your flight help your visualization and preparation?

chapter 21

Utilizing Dreams

chapter goals:

To address the importance dreams have in setting a positive environment for a successful flight.

To learn how to use your dreams to direct a positive flight from start to finish.

To help you to become more educated about the ongoing research on dreams.

Dreams can help you set goals, deal with unfulfilled wishes, make plans and practice a positive outcome for any event. This is an area others have not utilized in fear of flying programs that I have used with my clients and it has yielded success. There are some scientists who have taken the position that dreams are basically meaningless. Yet there are more and more professionals (psychologists, therapists, counselors, etc.) who are claiming positive outcomes for patients in therapy. Dreams give a wealth of information about what is going on in an individual's waking world, but it's what you do with that information that is essential. It is helpful to understand how dreams work, especially lucid dreams.

Understanding How Dreams Can Help

I've used dream analysis to help many clients uncover their fears, phobias and the underlying problems contributing to their fear of flying.

Exploring your dreams can help you reach self-awareness and gain insight. Dreams can be used as therapeutic tools that can help resolve an individual's problem with a fearful object, situation or anything of discomfort. After dream analysis, my clients have demonstrated success with public speaking, job interviews, relationship issues, health concerns and phobias like fear of flying.

After a dream, many individuals wonder why they had the dream, what it meant and what they should do about it. What are dreams? Dreams are mental activities that occur during sleep. Most dreams occur in conjunction with rapid eye movement or REM sleep (20 to 25 percent of your sleep).The act of dreaming is physical; the contents of dreams are psychological. It is better to find individual meaning rather than to depend on what a therapist or a dream dictionary tells you. It would take an entire book to thoroughly cover dreams, but for the purpose of this book we will cover what you will need to help you with your fear of flying.

I have found the Hill Cognitive-Experiential Dream Model very helpful in analyzing dreams.[1] This will help you recall your dreams in more vivid detail. The model is easy to follow and offers constructive steps for exploration, insight and action. I use an eclectic approach in theory orientation, so I appreciate the way the Hill model applies various theories: client-centered for the theoretical groundwork in the exploration stage, psychodynamic dream theory for the insight stage and behavioral theory for the action stage. It facilitates understanding of dreams and applies a process whereby your therapist collaborates with you to make changes in your waking life. It doesn't pressure you and helps to guide you in searching for your own personal meaning for the symbols in your dreams. We'll look at the Hill model a little later.

Many report difficulty in recalling their dreams. Keep a "Dream Journal" beside your bed and, when you awake from a dream, immediately write it down with all the details. Though you may be tired when you awaken from a dream, you must write it down, because even though it may have been very vivid you will be surprised at just how much you forget if you go back to sleep or wait until later in the day. It also helps to draw or paint your dream, especially a vivid scene that can give you powerful messages. A palpable picture permits you to reach more insight and associate the images with your waking life.

Hill's Three-Stage Model for Interpreting Dreams

1. **Exploration Stage:** To examine the individual images of the dream. It is important to re-experience the thoughts and emotions in the dream. If the dream is upsetting or stressful, use your relaxation techniques and exercises as you did for systematic desensitization. In some extremely emotional or difficult dreams it helps to work with a therapist.
2. **Insight Stage:** To understand your dream. This is where a therapist and client would collaborate to gain understanding of a dream.
3. **Action Stage**: To use what you have learned for making changes in your waking life.

Dream Interpretation Example

Michelle, a Catholic high school teacher, described a dream from her dream diary:

"I am kneeling in church and a small, clear plastic envelope falls out from my front, bottom tooth. The plastic envelope has become extraordinarily large in size and has a dime in it. My teeth feel exceptionally clean as if I have just come from a dental cleaning. I can hear the choir singing and I feel very happy. There is a bright light shining down and a golden cross above the altar. An angel is singing. I see her wings and they are beautiful; she seems to be my guardian angel. I feel at peace as I awaken."

Images: (what is remembered and interpretation of meaning)

- **Falling:** "I interpret this envelope as myself, descending into the unconscious, where I gathered valuable information regarding my tooth and seeing a dentist."
- **Dime:** "I interpret this as making a call to the dentist."
- **Tooth:** "I interpret this as a spiritual image, such as God guiding me with a message."
- **Cross:** "I interpret this as God and prayer. I feel it is a confirmation of my prayers."
- **Angel:** "I interpret this as a messenger of God, providing me with comfort."

- **Choir:** "I interpret this as saints and my guardian angel helping to pray for me."
- **Wings:** "I interpret this as freedom and my ability to achieve my flight on the plane; my guardian angel is protecting me."

Exploration Stage (**DRAW—D**escription, **R**e-experiencing, **A**ssociation, **W**aking Life Triggers)

- **Description:** "I am kneeling in church..."
- **Re-experiencing:** "Happy, calm, a feeling of relief, freedom, protection..."
- **Association:** "Feeling relief as the envelope leaves my tooth. The cross, the angel and the choir singing made me feel comforted and happy. I wasn't afraid."
- **Waking Life Triggers:** "We just moved into a new condo and I feel relieved that the move is over. When I went to bed, my tooth felt funny. I ate cashew nuts and bit down too hard. I've been afraid to fly and have scheduled my flight. Before going to bed, I was reading about *Waking Dreams* and asked my guardian angel to visit my dream."

Insight Stage:

- **Middle Level:** "This dream relates to my tooth hurting before going to sleep. The comfort that I get from God and my faith, attending church. The peace I feel from a spiritual presence."
- **Deepest Level:** "The dream relates to my learning to let go. The dime represents a message from my guardian angel, a spirit communicating to comfort me. Perhaps the dime is a message to call my dentist and make an appointment. The choir feels like the saints and my guardian angel are helping me pray. I believe the cross and church were comforting me from early childhood on, as I was raised Catholic. My guardian angel's wings were beautiful and made me feel free to fly."

Action Stage:

- "After gathering insight about the dream from my interpretation using the Hill model, I sense a direction for action to make changes. I have been procrastinating and afraid to make a dental appointment. I will search for dental insurance and make an appointment. It is a reminder to me to thank my guardian angel for communicating with me. The wings made me feel free and by working on my fear of flying, using my exercises, knowing I'll be safe, I can feel free to fly without my fear. I believe this dream helped me understand that I need to try harder to listen to my body's needs, face my fears and see the spiritual messages in my dreams."

Daily Activity: (Positives in my life, prior to the dream)

- I completed my work assignments.
- I read a book on dreams and communicating with my spiritual side.
- I ordered dinner instead of cooking.
- Working on my fear of flying, I felt more confident.

Daily Activity: (Negatives in my life, prior to the dream)

- My tooth was hurting.
- Trying to cut costs; the economy is hurting us.
- Wishing I didn't have to fly.

My Dream Interpretation

Start journaling. You may use a dream dictionary, but use your own meaning for symbols, too! This exercise demonstrates how to interpret your dreams and how to use the information that's uncovered.

My Dream:

____

Images: (what is remembered and interpretation of meaning)

____

____

____

____

____

____

____

____

Exploration Stage:

- Description:______________________________
- Re-experiencing: ___________________________
- Association:______________________________
- Waking Life Triggers: _______________________

Insight Stage:

- Middle Level: ____________________________
- Deepest Level: ___________________________

Action Stage:

- ______________________________________

Daily Activity: (Positives in my life, prior to the dream)

- ______________________________________
- ______________________________________
- ______________________________________
- ______________________________________
- ______________________________________

Daily Activity: (Negatives in my life, prior to the dream)

- ______________________________________
- ______________________________________
- ______________________________________
- ______________________________________
- ______________________________________

Lucid Dreams

Lucid dreams are dreams that give the dreamer awareness and control over his or her dream. They are dreams that help you rehearse or practice for an upcoming event like a game, a speech or your flight on an airplane. A lucid dream is when you awake within your dream or when you become aware that you are dreaming. You have the ability to make changes to your lucid dreams. These dreams are a state of consciousness in between waking and sleeping. Lucid dreams can be quite vivid. When you move between REM (rapid eye movement) and NREM (non-rapid eye movement) sleep, you can experience lucid dreams in which you are aware that you are dreaming. Prior to falling to sleep, you can decide what to dream within a lucid dream. Many influential people, athletes and celebrities have used the power of visualization to enhance their careers and achieve their life's dreams.

Many celebrities and athletes like Tiger Woods, Oprah Winfrey, Lebron James and Arnold Schwarzenegger have used their dreams to visualize success. Visualization techniques can be intensified when you start to make the images more vivid, add smell, movement and sound. There are individuals who thought they could never master the techniques of lucid dreaming but have done so with practice. I have had clients claim that specific foods can encourage lucid dreaming if eaten prior to bedtime; among these are dairy products, orange juice, pizza, mustard, ice cream, popcorn, pickles, fish, pork, hot dogs and heavy fried foods. Most food consumed before bed has been proven to make individuals dream, but it is also not a healthy practice to follow!

Dreams are an expression of consciousness while sleeping. You can use lucid dreams to face your anxiety, such as fear of flying or preparing for surgery or a contest, by practicing a routine with a positive outcome. You can become good at lucid dreaming with practice, belief and a positive attitude. Lucid dreams are more memorable.

Many individuals have the ability to program the content of their dreams before falling to sleep, but they cannot affect the dream when they are in it. Remember, all dreams have meaning and value.

Tips for Recalling Your Dreams

1. Before you go to bed, keep a clear mind. Tell yourself, "I will remember my dream when I awaken."

2. Plan to sleep between six and eight hours.
3. Avoid alcohol, taking medication or eating too close to your bedtime. (Although not a healthy habit to follow, you can try some of the specific foods individuals have found helpful for *lucid dreams*: dairy products, orange juice, pizza, mustard, ice cream, popcorn, pickles, fish, pork, hot dogs and heavy fried foods.)
4. Keep a pen and notebook (dream journal) or recorder next to your bed, so you can reach it as soon as you're awake.
5. Don't get out of bed immediately upon waking from a dream; lay still and keep your eyes closed, waking up slowly and trying to stay relaxed. Hold on to the feelings and let your mind relive the images/symbols (e.g., happy, sad, frightened, angry, etc.). Try to recall color and scents if you had any.
6. Write down as much detail as you can, even if it doesn't make sense.
7. Draw pictures to help recall details of your dream.
8. Talk to others about your dream so it is easier to remember the details.
9. Don't get discouraged. Eventually dream recall will come easily and you will be able to use messages from your dreams in your waking life.

Directing a Positive Flight

Using the information we have discussed, you can now be the director of your own flight. You can do so by using visualization, lucid dreaming and seeing yourself flying fear free. You are in control of your mind and your mind controls your body! Dream analysis is neither absolute nor perfect, but remember, when a situation doesn't turn out as you hoped, you can turn the negative into a positive and move forward. So start envisioning yourself succeeding in air travel. Write down the script and act it out, over and over.

Creating Positive Energy

It is easier to dwell on the negative than to apply energy to turn it around into a positive. I've observed that most of my clients wanted to be successful but didn't know how. When in doubt, do the best you can, stay focused and calm and do what you can while keeping a positive mind. Redirect your negative energy into doing something positive: exercise, journaling, reading, etc.

Points to Remember

There are some scientists who have taken the position that dreams are basically meaningless, but more and more professionals in psychology, therapy and counseling claim positive outcomes from dream therapy. Understanding your dream can help you reach self-awareness and gain insight. Dreams can be used as therapeutic tools, which can help resolve an individual's problem with a fearful object, situation or anything of discomfort. After a dream, many people wonder why they had the dream, what it meant and what they should do about it.

Dreams are mental activities which occur during sleep. The Hill Cognitive-Experiential Dream Model is very helpful in analyzing dreams. You will be able to recall your dreams in more vivid detail. The model is easy to follow and offers beneficial steps for exploration, insight and action.

A lucid dream is when you awake within your dream or when you become aware that you are dreaming. You have the ability to make changes within your lucid dreams.

You can be the director of your own flight by using visualization, lucid dreams and seeing yourself flying fear free. You are in control of your mind and your mind controls your body! Redirect your negative energy into doing something positive like exercising, writing or reading.

Key Questions

1. When and about what should you write in your dream journal?
2. How can you use dream therapy and visualization to improve other aspects of your life?
3. Do you feel confident that working with your dreams can help you overcome the fear of flying? Why or why not?

PART IV

Answers to Special Flight Fear Problems

chapter 22

When Self-Help Is Not Enough

chapter goal:

To explore additional possibilities when self-help is not enough for you.

Be aware that any program takes work and you must be willing to apply what you read and learn about to make these things work successfully for you.

For many, this self-help book, which utilizes an eclectic approach, will teach you how to undertake flying without fear. But for those who may need more help, Cognitive-Behavioral Therapy (CBT) has been the most successful treatment for fear of flying. New models and other techniques that are also effective in treating flight fear are: a systems approach, alternative methods, aromatherapy, music and color, computer games, dreams and diet.

There are various programs run by pilots and airlines that have proven beneficial for fearful flyers. There are also homeopathic and natural aid programs as well as medications, hypnotism, yoga, distraction, positive thinking and self-talk. The newest technique with reported success is Thought Field Therapy (TFT), developed by Roger Callahan, Ph.D. It is an alternative and currently non-validated psychotherapy treatment that taps various parts of the body to rebalance its natural energy system.

For those with certain psychological disorders or illnesses, self-help may not be effective. Medical treatments or antipsychotic drugs such as tranquilizers may be needed. People with panic disorders usually need to seek individual therapy and treatment that includes medication. When self-help is not working or symptoms are out of control, one should seek professional help for individual treatment. This chapter contains detailed suggestions about where to go to get help.

Seeking Professional Help

If you are experiencing medical symptoms or need a referral for your fear or phobias, you can consult your family physician. Here are other types of professionals who can help:

Psychologists

Many psychologists hold doctorate degrees, usually a Ph.D. or Psy.D., in psychology. Their mental health knowledge is comprehensive and they practice all the different types of psychotherapy and counseling. Various psychotherapies are: *Psychodynamic* (insight) *therapy* explores the unconscious dynamics of personality; *Behavioral therapy* focuses on changing maladaptive behavior by educating and using techniques; *Cognitive therapy* focuses on changing unrealistic beliefs; *Cognitive-behavioral therapy* integrates cognitive and behavioral techniques based on the belief that thoughts, moods and behaviors are interrelated; and *Family* and *Group therapies.* Therapists who incorporate bits from all therapies, focusing on which will be most effective for the individual, use an *eclectic* approach.

Psychologists are trained to make psychiatric diagnoses and provide psychological testing. They often consult with your family physician to better treat you, especially when medications may be needed.

Psychiatrists (MD or DO)

Psychiatrists are medical or osteopathic doctors who specialize in psychiatry. Their extensive training is generally needed to treat severe mental illnesses such as schizophrenia, bipolar disorder, major depression or panic disorder. Psychiatrists' main form of treatment is medication. In a few cases, some psychiatrists practice psychotherapy or marital counseling.

Licensed Professional Clinical Counselors (LPCC) and Licensed Professional Counselors (LPC)

Licensed professional counselors provide mental health and substance abuse counseling. Regulations and qualification requirements vary by state, so LPCCs may have extensive work experience and licensure testing. Licensed professional counselors hold master's degrees and are trained to provide individual, family and group counseling. LPCs diagnose and treat mental, behavioral and emotional problems and disorders, including addictive disorders; use psycho-educational techniques aimed at the prevention of such disorders; consult individuals, couples, families, groups and organizations; and conduct research into more effective therapeutic treatment modalities.[1]

Social Workers (LCSW)(LSW)(LMSWs)

Social workers hold master's degrees in social work. They provide counseling and psychotherapy. They have knowledge of community resources and work with community institutions and support systems. Social workers have different requirements and titles from state to state; some hold licenses and some do not hold master's degrees. There are many ways to locate a social worker. For suggestions, you can go to **www.helppro.com/nasw/BasicSearch.aspx**.

Pastoral Counselor

Pastoral counselors work for their churches or places of worship and do not charge a fee. There are also pastoral counselors who may or may not serve specific congregations, who hold graduate level or Ph.D. ministry degrees, counseling training, state licensing and/or certifications from an acknowledged counseling association. Several also hold counseling and psychology degrees. Pastoral counseling is available to anyone; you do not have to be a member of any church or specific denomination.

There are other professionals who also can be helpful, such as specialists on the topic: airline programs, pilots, seminars, etc. See a professional who is trained in working with the fear of flying. Make sure that you have a program with which you feel comfortable.

The next exercise will help you evaluate your progress with self-help to deal with your fear of flying. Self-assessment is beneficial to discover what is working and to make changes as needed. Be honest with yourself in doing this exercise.

Examining My Progress

What is working: ______________________________

____

____

____

____

____

____

What I might try: ______________________________

____

____

____

____

____

____

Professional Treatment and Research

With the extremely low number of problematic incidents in air travel, researchers are searching for the explanation of why an estimated 10 to 40 percent of the population suffer from the fear of flying. However, recent research has shown that one can overcome fear of flying with a brief treatment program; finding the main component to overcoming the fear and becoming clear about what is expected when one flies are important steps to success.

One of the most effective techniques for the treatment of fear of flying is *exposure therapy,* which involves making individuals face what they fear. The goal is *habituation,* a type of learning in which a response to a stimulus diminishes with repeated contact.

Several studies have been conducted on the fear of flying and, as time moves forward, hopefully there will be more empirical studies. *Blind studies, placebo responses, crossover studies* and *randomized studies* are used to reduce bias. In *blind studies,* either the observers or the subjects are kept ignorant of the group to which the subjects are assigned. In *placebo responses,* people receiving the placebo are the control group; those receiving the treatment or active drug are the experimental group. In *crossover studies,* subjects are randomly assigned to one of two groups. Because subjects in both groups received both treatment and placebo, each acts as his or her own control. In *randomization,* to ensure that the proportion of sick and healthy individuals is the same throughout the testing, individuals are randomly assigned and the number of individuals in each group does not need to equal the other.[2]

Studies have shown that agoraphobics avoid air travel due to their fear of having a panic attack in-flight, while simple phobics avoid air travel due to the fear of crashing. Oddly enough, agoraphobics worried little about plane crashes, but simple phobics worried the least about panic.[3] More research on this noteworthy theory still needs to be conducted.

Captain T.W. Cummings, a retired Pan Am senior pilot, is considered one of America's leading authorities on the fear of flying. Many agree with Cummings, who believes, "Fortunately, fear of flying—like most phobias—is among the most treatable of emotional problems." Cummings thinks that it is important to understand the facts of air travel and safety and to learn techniques in order to overcome the fear of flying.

I've had clients who have tried hypnosis and have had little to no success. Yet after using the techniques and exercises in this book and working with my program, they demonstrated 100 percent success and are flying free of fear. Capt. Tom Bunn, LCSW, founder and president of SOAR, Inc., points out:

"Hypnotism? It can work, but it depends upon the ability of the practitioner to know how to treat fear of flying without hypnosis. Simple relaxation-oriented hypnosis will not work; but linking each moment of flight to a moment of profound calming my work. Since a person can't tell whether the hypnotist knows how to do this, hypnosis is a hit or miss proposition for a fearful flier."[4]

Anti-Anxiety Medication

Many fearful flyers self-medicate with alcohol. More than 60 percent of fearful fliers use sedatives or alcohol to try to reduce their fear, according to a Stanford University study.[5] Jerilyn Ross, president of the Anxiety Disorders Association of America, claims that alcohol may serve as a temporary relaxant for fearful fliers but that it also makes them anxious and interferes with business travelers' ability to work after landing. According to Ross, a prescribed medication may relax a fearful flier who only flies occasionally but it is not the answer for long-term treatment of the problem.[6]

A study which was conducted at the Stanford University School of Medicine tested whether the anti-anxiety sedative-hypnotic medication benzodiazepine would help flight phobics. Results indicated that the medication increased physiological activation under acute stress conditions and hindered the therapeutic effects of exposure in those with flying phobias.[7] Instead of relieving the symptoms, when the medication suddenly "kicked in" during such a stressful situation it actually made the effects worse.

Also, Captain Tom Bunn, of whom we spoke earlier, finds that "Medications such as [benzodiazepine] increase panic when flying, and not just slightly, but by a factor of ten, according to research at Stanford University Medical School. The problem is terror. When taking meds, the ability to distinguish between what one fears and what is happening is lost, and what one imagines might happen is experienced [as actually] happening. Thus, panic and terror. And yet, after the flight, the person taking meds doesn't realize their terror was imaginary. They instead believed they lived through a life-threatening experience and were able to [survive] only because they were on meds (though that was what caused their "life-threatening" misadventure). So they continue taking meds until so traumatized they have to stop flying."[8]

The APA found evidence that proper and effective medications can be a part of the treatment plan for those who suffer from anxiety disorders and should be managed collaboratively by the individual's physician and therapist. But individuals should understand that there may be side effects to any drug. Also, the APA points out that treatment for anxiety disorders is not instantly effective:

"No one plan works well for all patients. Treatment needs to be tailored to the needs of the patient and to the type of disorder, or disorders, from which the individual suffers. A therapist and patient should work together to assess whether a treatment plan seems to be on track. Adjustments to the plan sometimes are necessary, since patients respond differently to treatment."[9]

Anti-anxiety medications can be helpful for individuals with severe symptoms and disorders, but you can work on your fear of flying with the information in this book, as empirical studies support that utilizing eclectic therapeutic methods with a multimodal approach is very effective for treating aerophobia.

Points to Remember

For those who may need individualized help, CBT has been the most successful model for treating the fear of flying. The American Psychological Association informs us of the important effects psychological support, CBT and an eclectic approach can have on the psyche, acute and long-term. Exposure through multiple modalities will be more successful in treatment of aviophobia.

There are several types of help that are available to you when self-help is not enough. If you are experiencing medical symptoms or you need a referral for your fear or phobias, you can consult your family physician. You can also contact psychologists, psychiatrists, counselors or social workers. There are others in the field who also can be helpful, such as specialists on the topic: airline programs, pilots, seminars, etc.

Studies have supported that fear of flying can be treated by multicomponent therapies such as self-help books, DVDs, hypnosis and virtual reality.

The APA found evidence that proper and effective medications can be a part of the treatment plan for those who suffer from anxiety disorders. These should be managed collaboratively by the individual's physician and therapist. But an important point that was made is that individuals should have an understanding that there may be side effects to any drug.

Anti-anxiety medications can be helpful for individuals with severe symptoms and disorders, but you also can work on your fear of flying with the information in this book, as empirical studies support that utilizing eclectic therapeutic methods with a multimodal approach is very effective for treating aerophobia.

Key Questions

1. When might self-help not work?
2. Can you name the professionals you can contact if self-help is not enough?
3. What treatment outside of self-help have you thought about using to end your flight fear?

chapter 23

Flying with Children

chapter goals:

To address your concerns and needs regarding flying pregnant and flying with newborns and children.

To explain the Lap Child Policy and child safety issues.

To cover general health and nutritional tips.

To learn to use various techniques in order to provide a positive flight for your children, answer their questions while remaining calm and staying in your parental role model position.

To create a bank of fun activities to use with children.

I have helped many children become relaxed flyers; I have discussed their surroundings with them, depending on their age, and given them activities that they can do while buckled in their seats, which makes the trip pass more quickly.

You want to be a good role model for your children, so relax and have fun with them! Answer their questions as you explain air travel procedures to them and let them know that security is for their safety, just as there are crossing guards at school, police officers and firefighters.

Depending on the ages of your children, it will help to teach them in age-appropriate ways what they may expect when they arrive at the airport. To illuminate the unknown for them, make at least one or two airport visits prior to your travel day, so they may see the airplanes and what they will be doing to prepare for their flight such as checking baggage, going through the security checkpoint, stopping at a shop to buy a cookie or enjoying a nice meal at one of the terminal restaurants.

Read a children's book about flying to your children one or two weeks prior to the flight; it will help them understand what to expect (e.g., *My First Airplane Ride,* by Patricia Hubbell). Also, role playing the experience with their friends can be fun. This will associate the playing experience with a positive flight, starting from making the reservation, to the airport procedures, the airplane ride, touchdown and arrival. Some moms and dads enhance the role playing: setting up a ticket counter and checking in their favorite suitcases, making a security checkpoint using a large cardboard box which they can walk through, arranging a sitting area at the gate, lining up chairs to make rows on the airplane and serving a fun lunch. Use your creative acting skills for the simulated flight and your artistic skills for setting up an air travel scene with realistic props. Make it fun!

Remember to keep your child's seat belt fastened throughout the entire flight and set a good example by keeping yours fastened too.

Traveling While Pregnant

Traveling pregnant isn't as bad as many soon-to-be mothers think! I worked as a flight attendant through the fifth month of my pregnancy and traveled by air up until my thirty-sixth week. Consult with your obstetrician prior to flying in an airplane when pregnant. Airlines vary on the cutoff period when you will not be permitted to fly during your pregnancy; most do not allow you to fly beyond thirty-six weeks domestically and not beyond thirty-two weeks internationally. According to the American College of Obstetricians and Gynecologists, air travel is safest for pregnant women during the second trimester, weeks eighteen to twenty-four. If you are considering a flight during your pregnancy, check with both your doctor and the airline before you book your flight.

Just as each woman is unique, so is each pregnancy. Alice, a client of mine, was in the twenty-fourth week of her pregnancy. Residing in Ohio, Alice was afraid to take a flight to Florida with her husband. Her obstetrician did not see a problem with her air travel, since she hadn't presented with any complications, but suggested a few tips to prepare for a healthy and comfortable flight. Nausea and fatigue are usually fleeting in the second trimester, but Alice had a few offbeat days. Alice followed her obstetrician's tips, which helped with her few episodes of nausea. Both air travel and pregnancy may cause swelling in the ankles and feet, so Alice wore a pair of larger size shoes, got out of her seat (which she booked close to the lavatories to make it more convenient) to stretch her legs and wore support hose for prevention of blood clots. Throughout the flight, Alice snacked lightly on salt-free pretzels and ginger snaps, used her sky blue and aquamarine color cards, took a few sniffs of mint leaves that she had put into a sachet pouch and drank plenty of water. Overall, Alice had a wonderful flight, making her husband happy that she could attend his award speech at his company's conference in Boca Raton, Florida.

Flying With a Newborn

The four common questions new parents have regarding flying with their newborns are:

1. *When will my baby be ready to take his or her first flight?* Consult with your child's pediatrician. Also, your baby shouldn't fly until he or she has received the first set of immunizations and has been fully examined for any congenital problems.
2. *Does my baby have to go through the X-ray screening machine?* The TSA has a wonderful website, **www.tsa.gov**, with videos you can view for traveling with children. The TSA states: "We have to screen everyone, regardless of age (even babies), before they can go through the security checkpoint. We will not ask you to do anything that will separate you from your child or children. We specially train our Security Officers and they understand your concern for your children. They will approach your children gently and treat them with respect. If your child becomes uncomfortable or upset, security officers will consult you about the best way to relieve your child's concern."[1] If a baby is carried through the metal detector in a carrier or sling, additional screening may be required whether there is an alarm or not. Remove babies and children from strollers or infant carriers so that the TSA security officers can screen them individually.
3. *How do I take my baby's breast milk through security?* The TSA has modified the rules associated with carrying breast milk through

security checkpoints. Mothers flying with or without their children are permitted to bring breast milk in quantities greater than three ounces, as long as it is declared for inspection at the security checkpoint. Breast milk is in the same category as liquid medications. You are encouraged to travel with only as much formula, breast milk or juice in your carry-on that will be needed to reach your destination. You are allowed to bring gel or liquid-filled teething rings, canned, jarred or processed baby food in your carry-on baggage and aboard your plane.

4. *I'm afraid of disturbing the other passengers if my baby cries. How do I keep him or her quiet?* First, don't be worried or embarrassed—babies cry and everyone knows it. Usually, newborns will sleep onboard the flight, but if they cry, you can give them their milk. Sometimes, infants may cry if their ears begin to hurt and that's a good thing; it can help unclog them, with the opening of their mouths. Also, giving them milk or a pacifier can help. Relax and so will your baby!

When you make your reservations, make sure you inform the agent that you are traveling with a newborn so that your seats will not be booked in an area that would not be permitted such as an exit row. The last row in first class or the first row in coach facing the bulkhead will give you more privacy and space. The downside is that it is difficult to watch in-flight entertainment if it's offered on your flight and there is no seat in front of you to stow your carry-on luggage; it must go up in the overhead compartment. If you select a window seat over the wings, the noise and vibration of the plane engines can help to put your infant to sleep, just like riding in the car does. You can also get a little privacy on that side for breastfeeding by turning your body a little towards the wall. You can book a window and aisle seat and hope that the middle seat remains open, but if it's a full flight you'll be out of luck. Some parents like to sit near the back of the plane so they are closer to the lavatories and the aft galley where one can stand and rock one's infant if he or she is crying. Remember, it is safer to remain in your seat with your baby in his or her CRS (Child/Infant Restraint System).

Check with the airline regarding its regulations for flying with a newborn baby. Some airlines no longer permit pre-boarding for parents and their children.

Health Tips for Pregnant Travelers

- Wear a pair of support hose and a larger size of shoes with adjustable straps, in case your feet swell. The support hose can help prevent DVT (Deep Vein Thrombosis), which can happen during pregnancy due to changes in your circulatory system and lack of calcium.
- Dehydration sometimes occurs when traveling on airplanes and can worsen when you're pregnant. Have plenty of water with you and avoid caffeine, alcohol and salt.
- Pack a few ginger tea bags or ginger tablets to help reduce nausea.
- Avoid carbonated beverages and gas-producing foods the day prior to and the day of your flight.
- Make sure to pack vitamin-rich fresh fruit such as apples, grapes, blueberries, plums, oranges or dried apricots and berries.
- Get up and walk around the cabin at least every two hours.
- Book your seat close to the lavatories for your convenience.
- Bring an eye mask and ear plugs so you can relax and rest. Rest as much as possible in-flight.
- Use easy, quick relaxation techniques, such as music and color therapy for a more restful flight.
- Wear loose, comfortable clothing. This will help with circulation.
- Take a sachet pouch of a pleasant scent so you can take a quick sniff in-flight, such as mint leaves to help with nausea, or if you notice a smell that may be unpleasant for you.
- BioBands are clinically proven wristbands that provide relief of nausea associated with travel (motion sickness) and pregnancy. You should consult with your obstetrician before using an acupressure wristband.
- Bring salt-free pretzels, ginger snaps and dry crackers to snack on every hour or in case you feel a little nausea.
- Try not to travel during your most uncomfortable hours; for instance, if you encounter nausea in the mornings, you should try to avoid booking morning flights.
- Don't lift your own carry-on to place it in the overheard compartment. Some gentleman or the flight attendants won't mind helping you. Don't be shy!

Traveling Safely with Children

The FAA and the National Highway Traffic Safety Administration (NHTSA) have agreed upon a single government performance standard that will satisfy both aviation and highway safety requirements for child/infant restraint systems.

If you're traveling with an infant under two years of age, it's a good idea to purchase a separate seat for your child and bring along a government-approved child safety seat. Strap the safety seat into the airline seat and your child into the safety seat, facing backwards. During the flight, if turbulence is encountered or in the unlikely event of an accident, your child will be much safer.

If your child is under the age of two, he or she may be held in an adult's lap or placed in a regular passenger seat for takeoff and landing. On international flights you're charged a fee for having a child in your lap. Check with your airline for their lap child policy; they can vary. Nevertheless, because of the safety benefits, the FAA encourages the use of approved child/infant restraints aboard aircraft. Holding a child on your lap is not safe. Turbulence can be unexpected and, no matter how much you love your child, you may not be able to hold on to him or her during an unexpected event like turbulence.

Child/Infant Restraint Systems (CRS)

- The CRS should have a solid back and seat,
- The CRS should have internal restraint straps installed to securely hold the child to the CRS,
- The CRS should be labeled stating that it has been approved for aviation use, and
- The CRS should have instructions on the label which must be followed (labels from other countries are allowed and thus may vary).

Your child restraint system must be installed in a forward-facing aircraft seat and in accordance with the instructions on the label. This includes placing the child restraint in either a forward- or aft-facing direction in the passenger seat. The CRS should not be installed in the same row as an emergency exit or in the row forward or aft of an emergency exit. A window seat is the preferred location; nevertheless, other locations may be acceptable, provided the CRS does not block any passenger's (including the parent or guardian of the child) way out to the aisle used to evacuate the aircraft. A responsible adult should occupy a seat next to the child.

During an emergency evacuation, the CRS should remain attached to the passenger seat and only the child should be removed from the aircraft.

Child Safety During Air Travel

Whether you are flying domestically or internationally, traveling with children requires patience, preparation and attention to safety issues. One of the most effective things you can do to promote your child's safe air travel is to listen to all announcements. For your safety and your child's, pay attention to the safety briefing, reading the safety card in the seat pocket in front of you and following instructions throughout the flight. Keep your child's seat belt fastened throughout the entire flight and set a good example by keeping your seat belt fastened too.

In preparing your children for air travel it helps to keep these points in mind:

- Remind them of the "No Talking to Strangers Rule." There are many individuals traveling through airports and you just don't know whom your child may meet.
- Instruct your children that if they need to, it's okay to speak to anyone working for the airline or a police officer.
- Make sure your child can say the name of the adult with whom he or she is traveling. It may help to write down your name on a small business card and place it in his or her pocket.
- Give everyone who is in your traveling party a picture of your child. A photo is a quick way of locating your child when missing.
- It helps to dress your traveling children in the same colored tops or caps. It makes it much easier to point out where everyone is and see that no one is missing from the party.
- Share a secret code word between the traveling parties so if needed, you can call out the word so your children can locate you.
- If the airline permits and you are traveling with another adult, pre-board to stow your luggage and secure the CRS.

Traveling with Children with Disabilities

Inform the airline when making your reservation if there are any special needs for your child. When going through the security checkpoint, inform the TSA officer if your child has any special needs or medical devices and what your child's abilities are (e.g., if your child can be hand-wanded, walk through the metal detector by him or herself or if he or she needs to be carried through the metal detector by the parent or guardian). If your child is unable to walk or stand, the TSA officer will conduct a pat-down search of your child, while he or she stays in his or her mobility aid, and will also conduct a visual and physical inspection of the equipment.

In-Flight Activities for Children

It makes the flight a positive and fun experience if you put together a backpack filled with small, wrapped activity items, giving one at a time to your child throughout the flight. The items don't have to be expensive. You can even pack a healthful snack. (Note: All toys should be quiet; avoid those that are noisy, sharp or that have several parts.)

Toys and activities for children to bring on an airplane can include:

- Books (preferably soft cover; new and favorites)
- Coloring/activity books (with odorless, non-toxic crayons)
- Sticker books
- Comic books
- Crossword puzzles
- A doll or stuffed animal (an airline figure is usually popular, like Flight Attendant Barbie or Captain Ken)
- Finger puppets
- Foam stickers
- Play flight attendant or captain kit
- Magnetic toys: maps, airport, etc.
- Foam puzzles: maps, airport, etc.
- CD or MP3 player with headphones
- New and favorite CDs
- Disposable camera (instruct not to use flash)

- ➢ Sitting exercises
- ➢ A diary (they can print/write their flight experience to share with friends or take to school for "Show and Tell")

A Few Helpful Tips:

- Pack colored sunglasses (preferably yellow). Neurologists have found that children with autism may be helped by wearing colored glasses (especially red), which counteract the over-firing of the high and mid brain. If the child is angry, orange or yellow appears to be more effective. Having the child put on a pair may quickly result in a calmer, more pleasant youngster.
- Blue colored real fruit gummies are calming.
- Ginger snaps help settle nausea.
- Provide a bottle of water, bought after the security checkpoint or on the plane (add one blue fizz candy to color the water to make it more calming and fun!).

Answering Your Child's Questions

How do you stay calm and be a good role model for your child if you're a fearful flyer? I've had many parents who haven't wanted their children to see them frightened or anxious for a flight. You now have many exercises, such as thought stopping, breathing exercises, color cards, etc., that you can use with your child. Be clear and answer your children's questions. You now understand the airline industry better and can respond intelligently to their concerns. It can be a learning experience for them.

Flying With Your Family

You want the flight to be fun, so use what you now know. Take family pictures and play games. Turn any negative into a positive. Use your exercises and techniques to stay focused and in control of the situation. Use self-talk: "I am going to have fun with my family! I can and I will! We are safe and enjoying our flight!"

It helps to let everyone share responsibilities on the flight so you are not stressed. Your children can handle their own carry-on backpacks, age permitting, thereby making them part of the team.

Buy everyone a disposable camera and build memories. The pictures will be fun to look at when you return home and for years down the road. You can also have everyone color a picture of their flight.

To keep other passengers happy while on the flight, play quiet games. To prevent your children from kicking the seats in front of them, attach pictures of someone or something they like to the back of the seats in front of them so they won't want to put their feet on them.

A fun family activity is to play games, such as looking around to see how many of something you can find (e.g., men with blue shirts, bald men, women with blonde hair, babies onboard, etc.) Stay focused, relax, have fun and make positive memories with your family!

Tips for Flying with Children

- If your child is ill, consult with your family physician to make sure he or she is well enough for the flight. For colds, increase liquids and vitamin C.
- On takeoff and landing, be sure to give your child a piece of gum to chew to prevent ear pain or blockage. For infants or toddlers, give them a bottle or a pacifier to suck on.
- If your infant or toddler is teething, this can be very painful, so pack a few teething rings (ask the flight attendant for a cup of ice to keep them cold), child's teething gel or consult your pediatrician for pain medication.
- As a precautionary measure, two weeks prior to your flight, try to limit your children's exposure to other children to prevent them from catching a cold or other illness.
- If your child is prone to motion sickness, as a precautionary measure, consult your pediatrician and check about one of the over-the-counter medications. Ginger snaps, herbal ginger tea, pretzels or dry crackers can soothe a nauseous tummy. Also, flying on an airplane is exciting for children and in combination with motion and possible turbulence, it's advisable that they travel on a light stomach.
- To help make it easier for your children to stay in their seats with their seat belts on, prepare activities to keep them busy and avoid sugar and junk food.

- Pack a children's waterless hand sanitizer, as well as instructing your children to wash their hands thoroughly when they visit lavatories on the plane and in the airport to prevent the spread of germs.
- Pack your own little "first aid kit" with items that your children may need, such as their allergy meds, asthma inhaler, vitamins, etc.
- Pack a pair of "Kids Character" slippers for in-flight comfort.

Unaccompanied Minors (UM)

The rules and restrictions for unaccompanied minors are different for each airline. Most airlines have a minimum age for their unaccompanied minor service, typically five, and a maximum age, typically twelve. Children younger than minimum age will have to travel with an adult. If your child appears to be older than the age limit set by the airline, you or your child may be asked to provide proof of the child's age, so be prepared to have appropriate documentation at the airport.

Rules for Older Children

If your child is older than an airline's maximum age for their unaccompanied child program, that airline may allow your child to travel under their program's rules, but your child may not be able to use special services for unaccompanied children such as having an escort while at the airport or being allowed to board the aircraft early.

Air Travel Restrictions

The number and type of restrictions vary by airline, as do additional fees for using this service. The usual restrictions may include:

- Your unaccompanied child is permitted only on nonstop flights.
- A higher minimum age is set if your child has to change planes.
- Your unaccompanied child is not permitted on the last flight of the day for that destination.
- Your unaccompanied child is not permitted on flights which include a second carrier.
- You may have to check in earlier, usually sixty to ninety minutes before departure.
- Adult fares or additional fees may be charged for unaccompanied children.

ID Requirements

Passengers under the age of eighteen are not required to have identification to get past security for domestic travel in the U.S. Depending on the airline, they may not be required to have identification to purchase a ticket or be issued a boarding pass. However, the adults who are responsible for a child at the departure and destination airports are required to have acceptable identification. While the airlines usually do not specify the identification required for the adult who drops off or picks up your child, the same kinds of government-issued photo identification that an adult uses for airline travel (for example, a driver's license or state-issued ID card) should be satisfactory.

Airline Supervision

Supervision for your unaccompanied child will vary by airline. Your child will likely be supervised by the flight attendants. Make sure that a flight attendant, preferably the head flight attendant, is aware of your unaccompanied child. Also, make sure that your child understands that if there is a problem during the flight that the flight attendant should be notified.

If your child has a connecting flight, make sure that he or she knows that he or she has to be escorted to the next flight by an airline representative. Once your child is in the waiting area, there may be an airline representative at that airport who will be responsible for supervising your child between flights, but that person most likely will have additional duties, including supervising other children. Make sure that your child understands the need to stay within sight of the responsible airline employee. If you feel that your child may not be able to deal with this kind of situation, then only book nonstop flights.

When a Flight is Diverted or Delayed

In the case of a delay or diversion, the airline will usually contact the person responsible for picking up or dropping off your child and make alternate flight arrangements. This may include arranging alternative transportation back to the original airport, arranging a later flight to the original destination or arranging a flight to an alternative airport where a responsible adult can pick up your child.

Regarding the airline's policies, if the flight is delayed overnight the airline may place your child in a hotel room alone or with another unaccompanied child under the supervision of an airline representative. The airline may also have a policy where it takes no responsibility for overnight stay for an unaccompanied child and will turn your child over to the local authorities for the night. It's imperative that you have a clear understanding of the airline's policies ahead of time.

When No One Picks Up Your Child

When there is no responsible adult at the destination airport, the procedure will depend on the airline's policies. The airline may try to contact the person who was to pick up your child and if there's a short wait, it will usually not be a problem. When no one can be contacted at the destination, then the responsible adult at the departure airport may be contacted to discuss alternatives. The airline should have several contact numbers for the responsible adult at both the departure and destination airports. When no one is available to take responsibility for the child, the airline may have to turn the child over to the local authorities.

International Flights

You may need to have additional documentation to allow your child to leave the departure country or to enter the destination country. Contact the appropriate authorities for each involved country to ensure that all requirements are being met.

Top Ten Safety Tips for Children Traveling Alone

1. Consider the maturity of your child.
2. Coordinate with whoever is picking up your child.
3. Tell your child what to expect during the flight.
4. Discuss appropriate behavior with your child.
5. Request appropriate seating.
6. Review airline polices.
7. Take extra precautions for connecting flights.
8. Spend extra time at the airport.
9. Identify and inform the head flight attendant.
10. Escort your child to his or her seat (if security allows).

New Pat-Down Procedures for Children

There have been several complaints regarding pat-downs (e.g., children upset and frightened, sexual harassment issues, etc.)

During a security pat-down of a six-year-old girl at the New Orleans airport, a video shot by her father seems to show a TSA agent putting her fingertips inside the waistband of the girl's pants as part of the pat-down procedure. This has contributed to the ongoing debate regarding TSA security procedures. A Utah congressman has proposed legislation to restrict pat-down searches of children.

In September 2011, United States Homeland Security Secretary Janet Napolitano said that children under 12 will not be required to remove their shoes and will be subjected to fewer pat-downs when going through airport security. TSA officers are being trained on the new procedures which are scheduled to be adopted nationwide.

Pat-downs are mainly used to make sure nothing prohibited is on a person's body, if an incongruity is detected during screening with advanced imaging technology (AIT) or during random screening. You will be given a pat-down before you're able to continue to your flight if there is suspicion or doubt. Pat-downs are also given to passengers who refuse screening by AIT or walk-through metal detectors.

There is usually a small percentage of passengers who need a pat-down. To avoid a pat-down at the checkpoint it helps to remove everything from your pockets prior to screening. Also, if you have an internal medical device, you will want to bring it to the TSA Officer's attention before screening.

Other points to remember:

- Pat-downs are conducted by same-gender officers.
- Every passenger has the right to request private screening at any point during the screening process.
- Everyone has the right to have a witness present during screening in the private screening area.

New screening systems for passengers will be implemented in the future. People may soon be allowed to keep their shoes, belts and other items on while passing through screening, due to improvements in technology.

Points to Remember

Depending on the age of your children, teach them what they can expect when they arrive at the airport. There are many activities you can do to prepare your children for their flight. It can lower your stress level if you and your children are ready. You and your children can have fun reading about and practicing the flight.

If you are pregnant, consult your obstetrician prior to flying. Airlines vary on the cutoff period when you will not be permitted to fly during your pregnancy. Most airlines do not allow pregnant women to fly beyond thirty-six weeks domestically and thirty-two weeks internationally. Wear support hose and a larger size of shoes, in case your feet swell. Have plenty of water with you and avoid caffeine, alcohol and salt. Pack a few ginger tea bags or ginger tablets to help reduce nausea.

When you make your reservations, make sure you inform the agent if you are traveling with a newborn, so that your seats will not be booked in an area where a newborn would not be permitted, such as an exit row.

In preparing your children for air travel, it helps to keep in mind child safety, such as reminding them of the "No Talking to Strangers Rule." It helps to dress your traveling children in the same colored tops or caps, etc. It makes it much easier to point out where everyone is and see that no one is missing from the party. When traveling with a child with disabilities, inform the airline when making your reservation if there are any special needs for your child.

It makes the flight a positive and fun experience if you put together a backpack filled with small, wrapped activity items.

You want to stay calm and be a good role model for your child. Answer your child's questions truthfully. On takeoff and landing, make sure to give your child a piece of gum to chew to prevent ear pain or blockage. For infants and toddlers, give them bottles or pacifiers to suck on.

It helps to know the rules and regulations for unaccompanied minors if your child must undertake air travel without you or another adult.

Key Questions

1. What precautions will you take when travelling with your children?
2. What security measures have been put in place so that children are safe when travelling by air?
3. What questions do you still have about travelling while pregnant or with young children?

Looking Ahead

Congratulations. You've learned many techniques and exercises that will help reduce your flight fear. Be confident. Practice what you've learned in this book and take it with you as you travel. Remember, overcoming fear requires work and it will take time to achieve your goals.

Use what you learned about the nature of your fear. Your fear is common and there are solutions to overcome that fear. Just by getting through this self-help book, you've helped yourself become a more courageous person.

Keep in mind the techniques and exercises that were introduced and explained in this book. Your Goodie Bag, your favorite colors, your favorite teas—all of these comforting items—will change as you get more comfortable taking air travel. Revisit the work you did in this book and track your progress. Not only will you recognize where you can improve, but you'll feel good seeing how far you've come to overcome your fear.

Most importantly, enjoy living a fear-free life. As I mentioned in the beginning, this book may or may not have been enough for you to overcome your fear, but I hope that it has at least given you the motivation and courage to begin the journey toward a happier future. Many of the fearful flyers I have helped have sent me postcards, letters and phone calls telling me how much their lives have changed since overcoming their fears. It's my sincere wish that you continue to grow and become more comfortable.

We can't control the airline industry. There will be changes. There will be incidents. And we can't control the situations that may require us to take air travel. But we can control ourselves and we can control our fear.

It is my hope that you will use the information in this book whenever you need it. Bring this book with you on flights and let it comfort you and give you confidence.

Remember to stay relaxed and positive. Good luck!

Quick Tips

- Prepare four or five days prior to your flight by taking Vitamin C, following a healthful, low sodium, low flatulence diet and leaving out greasy, sugary foods and avoiding alcohol, caffeine and carbonated beverages.
- For extra leg comfort, book an aisle seat or request the exit row if you meet the qualifications to be an able bodied passenger (ABP).
- On longer flights, get up occasionally and walk around, at least once every two hours. Sitting for lengthy periods of time may cause blood clots in your legs.
- If you have a cold or suffer from allergies, take a decongestant about thirty minutes prior to the flight. This can help shrink your sinus membranes. Also, using a saline nasal spray can be helpful.
- If you worry about your ears blocking, chew gum and yawn on takeoff and descent.
- Plane cabins can be very hot, especially prior to takeoff (sitting on the tarmac or while taxiing) and they can become quite cold at high altitudes, especially on night flights. Bring a jacket or sweater; it helps to layer your clothes. Once you get settled in your seat, ask the flight attendant for a pillow and blanket. (You may be lucky and get one, if you ask before they're all handed out!)
- Due to low air pressure and altitude, your feet may swell, especially if you take off your shoes. Wear larger comfortable shoes that slip on and wiggle your toes! Some individuals like to bring a comfortable pair of slippers to put on while in-flight.
- Stay hydrated; drink plenty of water. Avoid alcohol, caffeine and carbonated beverages. These beverages will dehydrate you due to the cabin's dry air.

- Bring a few healthful snacks such as low-salt pretzels, granola bars, nuts, etc.
- Put together your Goodie Bag, filled with magazines, color cards, playing cards, games, pictures, relaxation items (color stones, aromatherapy, music, comic books, entertaining books to read, this book, etc.). You may wish to bring your own headphones, but remember you want to travel light! To block out sound and light, bring earplugs or noise-reducing headphones and a blindfold or colored glasses.

Reflection

Take time to reflect when doing this last exercise. Recognize where you started with your fear and where you are now. Assess your progress in accomplishing your goals and set new goals for yourself.

Acknowledgements

I am grateful to the staff at New Horizon Press for their support and help in turning my work into the creation of this book. I want to acknowledge those individuals who were in my study and worked courageously on their fear of flying. They shared their stories and anxious behaviors due to the fear of flying that negatively affected their lives in many ways. My clients devoted their time, learned the techniques, practiced the exercises and confronted their fears. I commend them for such motivation and success. I am proud of the many students who believed in my program, took my classes, attended lectures and workshops and successfully fly more comfortably without fear.

I am grateful to clinical psychologist, instructor, mentor and author Dr. Jonathan Rich for his encouragement and guidance on my proposal and work. I am indeed grateful to my publisher and editor-in-chief, Dr. Joan Dunphy, vice president JoAnne Thomas and production editor Charley Nasta for their expertise and faith in me and my book's message. A special thanks goes out to cover designer Wendy Bass and interior designer Susan Sanderson for their creative talents.

Appendix A: The Color Chart

Absorb Your Energy Color!

Refer to the small color samples on the back cover of this book. You can also explore color therapy and color charts online at **www.holisticonline.com/color/color_home.htm**, **http://www.therapycolor.com** and **www.colorquiz.com/about.html**.

1. WHITE: calming, focusing, hope, integrity, idealistic, clean (can drain energy)
2. TURQUOISE: soothes emotional shock, helps you get on with your life, assertiveness, goal setting, perception, prosperity
3. GREY: soothing, weak, clouded, bland
4. SILVER: calming, restores equilibrium, emotional tranquilizer
5. PURPLE: strong relaxation to depressed mood, respect, proud, distinguished
6. BLACK: introverted, closed personality, depressed mood, self-confidence, power, strength, high discipline and a feeling of freedom
7. LAVENDER: calming, relaxation, peacefulness, rested and aristocratic attitude
8. DARK GREEN: remorse, resentment, possessiveness
9. GREEN: soothing, relaxing mentally as well as physically, helps those suffering from depression, helps fatigue, soothes headaches, helps with claustrophobia, anxiety, nervousness
10. EMERALD GREEN: easygoing, wealth
11. JADE: balanced, wisdom, generosity of spirit
12. AQUAMARINE: picks up spirits, meditation, calming, peacefulness
13. MINT GREEN: alertness, soothing, focusing
14. PALE GREEN: immaturity, fresh start, indecisive
15. BLUE: wholeness, communication, balance, cooling, calming, lowers blood pressure, slows down, retarding growth and decreasing respiration, inventor insight (negative effect during depressed mood with dark blue)

16. BLUEBERRY BLUE: memory, balance, cooling, healing
17. INDIGO: relaxes, provides a peaceful environment, radiant energy
18. AZURE BLUE: happiness, satisfaction with purpose, stability, calmness, cool
19. OCEAN BLUE: relaxation, openness, easy breathing, cooling, refreshing, strength, tranquility
20. SKY BLUE: calming, conquer hurdles, cooling, openness, peacefulness
21. PALE BLUE: determined to succeed, uplifting, ambitious, giving, relaxing
22. YELLOW: energizes, relieves depression, low self-esteem, gloom, improves memory, stimulates appetite, self-esteem booster, can help with fears and phobias
23. LEMON YELLOW: orderly, wisdom
24. PRIMROSE YELLOW: exploring, supersensitive, sensitive
25. CREAM: reassurance, stretching of space, casualness, laxity
26. GOLD: helps with physical and psychological depression, uplifting
27. ORANGE: energizes, stimulates appetite and digestive system
28. PEACH: immaculate behavior, helps communication
29. RUBY RED: express powerful feelings, warm, passion
30. MAROON: cautious, overcome difficulty, thoughtfulness
31. MAGENTA: spirituality, uplifting, negotiator
32. CRIMSON: wealth, social standing, religious, power, importance, aggressive
33. SCARLET: willingness, love, power, academics, theology, warmth
34. MAUVE: making right choices, noble, ruling
35. PINK: compassionate, faithful, trusting, nurturing, relaxes muscles, tranquil, relieves tension and soothing, calming within minutes of exposure, suppresses hostile, aggressive and anxious behavior

Notes

Chapter 1

1. "Specific Phobias," last modified July 13, 2011, National Institute of Mental Health, http://psychcentral.com/lib/2006/specific-phobias/.
2. Duane Brown, *Flying Without Fear* (Oakland, CA: New Harbinger Publications, Inc., 2008), 105.
3. Sadie F. Dingfelder, "Fear itself," *Monitor on Psychology* 37 (2006): 22.
4. David Carbonell, "Fear of Flying?", Anxiety Coach, http://www.anxietycoach.com/fearofflying.html (accessed July 25, 2010).
5. Barbara Fadem, *Behavioral Science, 4th Ed.* (Baltimore, MD: Lippincott Williams & Wilkins, 2008), 120.
6. Frank H. Wilhelm and Walton T. Roth, "Clinical characteristics of flight phobia," *Journal of Anxiety Disorders* 11 (1997): 241-261.
7. Gary Stoller, "Fear of flying can cripple workers," *USA Today*, http://www.usatoday.com/educate/college/business/articles/20060326.htm (accessed September 19, 2010).

Chapter 2

1. David Parker Brown, "By the Numbers, Flying is a lot Safer than Driving or Taking the Train," Airline Reporter, http://www.airlinereporter.com/tag/fear-of-flying/ (accessed November 11, 2011).
2. Brenda K. Wiederhold and Mark D.Wiederhold, "Side effects and contraindications," in *Virtual Reality Therapy for Anxiety Disorders*, (Washington, DC: American Psychological Press, 2005).
3. Jack Curry, "Why Plane Crashes Happen," *International Herald-Tribune*, July 19, 2009, 12.

Chapter 3

1. Pamela Griffiths, "Fear of flying," *Therapy Today* 18 (2007): 32-34.
2. Richard Rayner, "Nowhere, U.S.A." *New York Times Magazine* 6, (1998): 42-46; Joe Sharkey, "Business travel; try to relax," *New York Times*, January 12, 2000.
3. Carbonell, "Fear of Flying?"
4. Sara Freedman and Rhonda Adessky, "Cognitive Behavior Therapy for Panic Disorder," *Israel Journal of Psychiatry and Related Sciences* 46, no. 4 (2009): 251-256.
5. Jeanine K. Stefanucci and Dennis R. Proffitt, "The roles of altitude and fear in the perception of Height," *Journal of Experimental Psychology: Human perception and performance* 35, no. 2 (2009): 424.
6. Chris Gordon, "Scared of Heights," *Psychiatric Times* 26 (2009): 1-3.

7. Ruth Hüweler, et al., "The impact of visual flow stimulation on anxiety, dizziness, and body sway in individuals with and without fear of heights," *Behaviour Research and Therapy* 47, no. 4 (2009): 345.
8. Brown, *Flying Without Fear*.

Chapter 4

1. "Boeing and Aviation Safety," Boeing, http://www.boeing.com/commercial/safety/faq.html (accessed November 11, 2011).
2. "Osama Bin Laden: Experts Fear Revenge By Al Qaeda or 'Lone Wolf'," ABC News/Yahoo News, http://abcnews.go.com/US/osama-bin-laden-triggers-security-alert-recall-marine/story?id=13505844#.TrwdP1awX0Q (accessed November 11, 2011).
3. "3-1-1 for Carry-Ons," Transportation Security Administration, http://www.tsa.gov/311/(accessed November 11, 2011).
4. "Former Miss USA Susie Castillo Felt 'Violated' by TSA Agent in Body Search," Fox Television Stations, Inc., http://www.myfoxboston.com/dpps/entertainment/former-miss-usa-susie-castillo-felt-violated-tsa-agent-dpgonc-20110429-fc_12981211(accessed November 11, 2011).
5. Patricia Reaney, "Travelers see security patdowns as necessary hassle," Thomson Reuters, http://www.reuters.com/article/2011/03/11/us-travel-security-idUSTRE72A3HX20110311?feedType=RSS&feedName=everything&virtualBrandChannel=11563 (accessed November 11, 2011).

Chapter 5

1. Michael Sand et al., "Surgical and medical emergencies on board European aircraft: a retrospective study of 10189 cases," *Critical Care* 13, (2009).
2. Melissa L. P. Mattison, MD and Mark Zeidel, MD, "Navigating the Challenges of In-flight Emergencies," JAMA, http://jama.ama-assn.org/content/early/2011/04/29/jama.2011.618.extract (accessed November 11, 2011).

Chapter 6

1. Terry Smiljanich, "New Information On Safest and Worst Domestic and Foreign Airlines," Consumer Warning Network, http://www.consumerwarningnetwork.com/?s=airline+safety (accessed November 12, 2011).

Chapter 7

1. Ed Sternstein and Todd Gold, *From Take-off to Landing* (New York: Pocket, 1990).
2. Roger C. Smith, "Stress, anxiety, and the Air Traffic Control Specialist: Some surprising conclusions from a decade of research," in *Stress and Anxiety*, ed. C.D. Spielberger, et al., Vol. 9 (New York: Hemisphere Publishing, 1985): 95-109.

3. "Electronic Code of Federal Regulations, Sec. 121.503," Federal Aviation Administration, http://ecfr.gpoaccess.gov/cgi/t/text/text-idx?c=ecfr&sid=33f60377d398dbaefc8a9a5dd0f37e34&rgn=div5&view=text&node=14:3.0.1.1.5&idno=14#14:3.0.1.1.5.19.3.2 (accessed November 11, 2011).
4. Smith, "Stress, anxiety, and the Air Traffic Control Specialist."
5. "Press Release - FAA Announces Additional Actions as Part of Air Traffic Control Review," FAA, http://www.faa.gov/news/press_releases/news_story.cfm?newsId=12682 (accessed November 11, 2011).
6. "Press Release - FAA and NATCA Reach Agreement on Fatigue Recommendations," FAA, http://www.faa.gov/news/press_releases/news_story.cfm?newsId=12883 (accessed November 11, 2011).
7. Mike M. Ahlers, "FAA proposes major revamp of airline pilot training," CNN Travel, http://articles.cnn.com/2011-05-11/travel/faa.pilot.training_1_colgan-air-flight-flight-attendants-faa?_s=PM:TRAVEL (accessed November 11, 2011).

Chapter 8

1. "Boeing and Aviation Safety, Frequently Asked Questions (FAQs)," Boeing, http://www.boeing.com/commercial/safety/faq.html#FAQ10 (accessed November 11, 2011).
2. "Advisory Circular 121-33B," FAA, http://rgl.faa.gov/Regulatory_and_Guidance_Library/rgAdvisoryCircular.nsf/list/AC%20121-33B/$FILE/AC121-33B.pdf (accessed November 11, 2011).

Chapter 15

1. Aymen Fares, "Color Therapy Then & Now - Part 2," Spiritual.com.au, http://www.spiritual.com.au/2011/07/color-therapy-then-now-2/ (accessed November 11, 2011).
2. Helen Graham, *Discover Color Therapy* (Berkeley, CA: Ulysses Press, 1998).
3. "Lüscher color test," Wikipedia, http://en.wikipedia.org/wiki/L%C3%BCscher_color_test (accessed November 11, 2011).
4. Arnold Wilkins, "Visual Stress in Neurological Disease," ACNR, http://www.acnr.co.uk/pdfs/volume4issue6/v4i6rehab.pdf (accessed November 11, 2011).

Chapter 17

1. "Prohibited Items For Travelers," Transportation Security Administration, http://www.tsa.gov/travelers/airtravel/prohibited/permitted-prohibited-items.shtm (accessed November 11, 2011).

Chapter 18

1. "ACSM In The News: Laugh a Little to Help Protect Heart, Lower Blood

Pressure," American College of Sports Medicine, http://www.acsm.org/about-acsm/media-room/acsm-in-the-news/2011/08/01/laugh-a-little-to-help-protect-heart-lower-blood-pressure (accessed November 11, 2011).

Chapter 20

1. "Wolpe, Joseph," New World Encyclopedia, http://www.newworldencyclopedia.org/entry/Joseph_Wolpe#Subjective_Units_of_Disturbance_Scale (accessed November 11, 2011).

Chapter 21

1. Clara E. Hill et al., "Working with dreams using the Hill cognitive-experimental model: A comparison of computer-assisted, therapist empathy, and therapist empathy + input conditions," *Journal of Counseling Psychology* 50, no. 2 (Apr 2003): 211-220.

Chapter 22

1. "Who are Licensed Professional Counselors?" American Counseling Association, accessed at www.counseling.org.
2. Fadem, *Behavioral Science*, 120.
3. Richard J. McNally and Christine E. Louro, "Fear of flying in agoraphobia and simple phobia: distinguishing features," *Journal of Anxiety Disorders* 6 (1992): 319-324.
4. Captain Tom Bunn, comment to " Flying without wings - Part 2," Emma Forbes, http://www.forbesstyle.com/flying-without-wings-pt2 (accessed November 11, 2011).
5. Wilhelm and Roth, "Clinical characteristics of flight phobia."
6. Libby Peacock, "A wing and a prayer," *SmartTravel*, http://www.smarttravelasia.com/printer/print.php (accessed September 9, 2010).
7. Frank H. Wilhelm and Walton T. Roth, "Acute and delayed effects of alprazolam on flight phobics during exposure," *Behaviour Research and Therapy* 35, no. 9 (September 1997): 831-841.
8. Captain Tom Bunn, answer to "Are you afraid to fly?", Yahoo Answers UK & Ireland, http://uk.answers.yahoo.com/question/index?qid=20100710082105AAxruIi (accessed November 11, 2011).
9. "Anxiety disorders and effective treatment," American Psychological Association, http://www.apa.org/helpcenter/anxiety-treatment.aspx (accessed November 12, 2011).

Chapter 23

1. "Traveling With Kids," Transportation Security Administration, http://www.tsa.gov/travelers/airtravel/children/index.shtm (accessed November 11, 2011).